A Lot Of Bull
About Kentucky

by Steve Talbott

TURNER PUBLISHING COMPANY

TURNER PUBLISHING COMPANY
412 Broadway • P.O. Box 3101
Paducah, Kentucky 42002-3101
(270) 443-0121

Turner Publishing Company Staff:
Dayna Spear Williams, Editor
Kristi Johnson, Editor

Library of Congress Control Number: 2001087463
ISBN: 1-56311-713-4

Printed in the United States of America. Additional copies
may be purchased directly from the publisher.
Limited Edition.

DEDICATION

I
am going
to dedicate this
masterful work of art
to the two people who have
motivated, influenced, inspired, driven,
excited, devoted, strengthened and fulfilled
my life –
my
two
best friends
and
twin daughters,
Shannon and Erica.

INTRODUCTION

This book is not a history book nor is it a scholarly work. It is simply an overview of Kentucky represented by photographs and trivial facts, which I hope you will find educational, interesting and perhaps even humorous at times. An effort has been made to cover the entire state from north to south and east to west through the four seasons.

This book has taken almost nine years to complete. Some of the photographs are of subjects that may or may not still exist. During the nine years of photographing, an attempt was made to select only the pictures that depict Kentucky as it is, the good as well as the bad, the well known as well as the hidden out-of-the-way places, the typical tourist stops, and even some places that most Kentuckians have never been to or heard of.

All 120 counties of Kentucky have been mentioned at least one time in this book, some more than others. I have tried to find interesting little tidbits about counties and communities and even some people themselves that the majority of Kentuckians have never thought about before.

Kentucky is not the largest state, nor the oldest, but it has a wealth of history and interesting places and people. There are places in Kentucky that are, quite frankly, eyesores, embarassments and the reason for a lot of stereotyping about this state and its people. On the other hand, Kentucky has some of the most beautiful scenery found anywhere in the world.

The greatest compliment this book could ever be paid, would be for someone to say "I didn't know that about Kentucky."

LOUISVILLE SKYLINE

The skyline of Kentucky's largest city stands out alongside the Ohio River. Notice anything missing? The Louisville floating fountain, largest in the world, is not there anymore. Seems it fell into disrepair and was removed from the river and is now sitting in storage somewhere. The good news is there is a picture of the floating fountain elsewhere in this book.

BET YOU DIDN'T KNOW...

From 1990 to 2000, the county that had the highest population growth rate was Spencer County with an increase of 73 percent. The county's population grew from 6,801 to 11,766.

Versailles, seat of Woodford County, is situated on the site of an earlier community which was named Falling Springs.

Cumberland Falls

Although not the highest falls in Kentucky, Cumberland Falls is the largest waterfall east of the Rockies and south of Niagara Falls. These falls are normally 125 feet wide and drop 68 feet.

Cumberland Falls is only one of two places in the western hemisphere that has a "moonbow." This is like a rainbow only it is visible at night when the moonlight shines on the mist in front of the falls. The only other place in the western hemisphere with this is Africa's Victoria Falls.

Bet you didn't know...

The community of Eubank, in Lincoln County, was the home of the 1944 Miss America.

In 1867, when two neighboring Campbell County communities, Jamestown and Brooklyn, had grown together, it became one town and was renamed Dayton.

FORT BOONESBOROUGH

"Fort Boone," as it was known then, began April 1, 1775 by Daniel Boone and some of his woodsmen. When completed in the summer of that year, it consisted of 26 one-story log cabins and four blockhouses arranged in a rectangle approximately 260 feet long and 180 feet wide.

Intended as the hub of a great colony, Fort Boonesborough did not last long. After the Revolutionary War ended and the fort was no longer needed for defense, its decline was rapid.

The population of the fort dwindled for several reasons. One being due to fear of Indian attack. Another reason the settlers left in disgust was because their land titles were worthless.

When the fort was passed over in its bid to become the county seat of Madison County and the state capital, many more left.

BET YOU DIDN'T KNOW...

The first issue of the *Louisville Courier-Journal* was Nov. 8, 1868.

FLORAL CLOCK

Adjacent to the state capital, this working clock is 34 feet in diameter and uses 20,000 plants in the face. The clock is tilted at an angle and is above a reflecting pool of water with three fountains in the front.

BET YOU DIDN'T KNOW...

Referring to Kentucky, the first use of the word "commonwealth" occurred in 1785 when the inhabitants of the newly-formed Kentucky District petitioned Virginia that it wanted to be known by the name of "Commonwealth of Kentucky" and to be recognized as a "free and independent state."

Bet you didn't know...

The first county seat of Oldham County was Westport, but, in 1827 it moved to LaGrange. The next year it moved back to Westport and in 1838 it moved back to LaGrange.

Dale Hollow State Resort Park has the largest concentration of deer in the Commonwealth of Kentucky.

Tiny axe-swinging prohibitionist Carrie Nation was born in Lancaster, seat of Garrard County.

Bet you didn't know...

Up until the time of the Civil War, Clarke County was spelled with an "e" on the end. The man for whom the town was named, George Rogers Clarke, also spelled his name with a final "e." The letter "e" on the end of some words, for example shoppe, began getting dropped from the spelling during the period from around 1850 to the end of the Civil War.

The first governor of Kentucky was Isaac Shelby. He was also the fifth governor.

Medieval Europe?

Nope, this castle can be found located in Woodford County right down the road from Bluegrass Field in Fayette County. And who says Kentucky doesn't have a little bit of everything?

Bet you didn't know...

Prior to July 18, 1922 Kentucky was only one of seven states that did not have a commercial radio station.

MOUNT ZION COVERED BRIDGE

Located outside of Springfield in Washington County, this bridge is 211 feet long and 16 feet wide and is one of the longest multi-spans in Kentucky

BET YOU DIDN'T KNOW...

Of the 47 state parks in Kentucky, only 14 are "resort" parks. In order to be a resort park, it must have a lodge and a restaurant.

Kentucky's motto is "United We Stand, Divided We Fall."

Bourbon County Courthouse

Bourbon County was named for the royal French family who aided the colonies in the War of Independence. Bourbon was one of nine Virginia counties formed before Kentucky became a state, actually a commonwealth in 1792. From its original area all of 24 counties and parts of 10 other new ones were made. At this site the first courthouse in 1787 marked the county seat.

Bet you didn't know...

All major waterways in Kentucky flow northward and northwest-ward to the Ohio River.

The Westvaco Paper Mill in Wickliffe manufactures some of the paper used in the cover of National Geographic Magazine.

THIS IS NOT A WAY OUT OF CARTER CAVES

What you see is not what you think it is. The trees you see in the opening are actually a reflection off of a pool of water. The opening is above the water and the angle is such that the image is reflected off the pool of water into the cave, making it look like you are heading for an exit. If the level of water varies more than a couple of inches, it will not reflect the image of the trees.

There are over 20 caverns in Carter Caves. Cascade Cave features an underground waterfall that is over 30 feet high.

BET YOU DIDN'T KNOW...

The Ohio River was formed approximately 10,000 years ago when the glaciers receded.

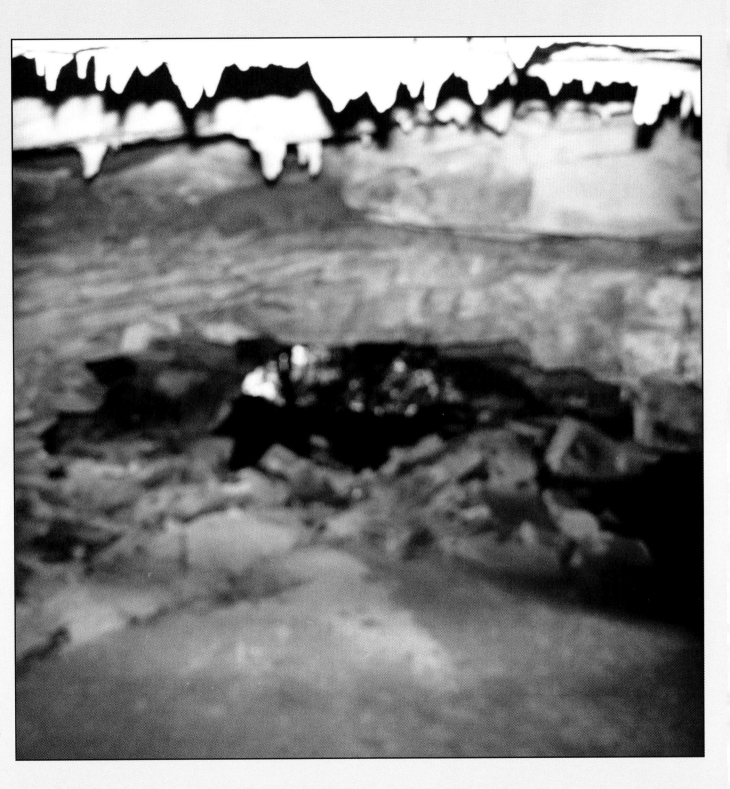

Turkey Vulture

Would you recognize a turkey vulture if you heard one? Probably not, because turkey vultures are in the family of American vultures, which are voiceless. They make no sound. These birds sport bald heads and curved beaks and live on a diet of decaying flesh (carrion).

Bet you didn't know...

Kentucky School for the Deaf in Danville, seat of Boyle County, was the first school of its kind in the nation.

BLUEGRASS FIELD

Known in Lexington as the Versailles Road, US 60W cuts between Bluegrass Field and Keeneland Racetrack as it winds westward toward Versailles in Woodford County.

Bluegrass Field has two runways. Runways are numbered according to the magnetic direction the airplane faces when lined up on the end for takeoff. The last zero is dropped so that, for example, runway 22 is actually facing 220 degrees. The opposite ends of runways are exactly 180 degrees apart, so the other end of runway 22 is runway four which faces 040 degrees. Since a circle has 360 degrees, the highest number a runway can have is 36. In aviation radio jargon, numbers are said individually so that runway 22 is called "runway two-two" and runway 36 would be called "runway three-six"

The long runway at Bluegrass Field is 4-22 and is 7,003 feet long and 150 feet wide and is the runway used most often. The shorter runway is 8-26 and like the examples above, one end faces 080 degrees or almost east and the opposite end faces 260 degrees.

Different ends of the runway are used since airplanes always land facing the wind.

ROEBLING SUSPENSION BRIDGE

Designed by John Roebling, who also designed the famous Brooklyn Bridge in New York City and High Bridge in Wilmore, KY this bridge connects Covington, KY to Cincinnati, OH. When this bridge opened Jan. 1, 1867 it was the longest suspension bridge in the world, spanning 1,057 feet.

BET YOU DIDN'T KNOW...

There are eight public and 28 private colleges and universities in Kentucky.

Motion picture and television star Ned Beatty was born in St. Matthews in Jefferson County in 1937. The following year in 1938, he won the "Best Breastfed Baby" contest.

BARGE ON THE MISSISSIPPI

This picture was taken while at the Columbus-Belmont State Park on the western end of Kentucky in Hickman County. Bordered by the mighty Mississippi River on its western edge, one can always see tugboats pushing barges up or downstream at all hours of the day

BET YOU DIDN'T KNOW...

More people visit Kentucky Dam Village State Park than any other state park in Kentucky.

Caldwell County was named after Gen. John Caldwell who fought in the 1786 Indian expedition. He later became Kentucky's lieutenant governor.

CONSTITUTION SQUARE

Located in Danville, Kentucky's first capital, is this reproduction of Kentucky's first courthouse square. This is also the site of the first post office in the West, built in 1792. On this site in 1784, the plans were made for Kentucky's independence from Virginia. In 1792, the first Kentucky constitution was drawn here.

BET YOU DIDN'T KNOW...

Boone County was Kentucky's 13th county to be formed.

There are 14 locks and dams on the Kentucky River.

KEENELAND

This thoroughbred track opened for business in 1936. Most of Keeneland's racing occurs during the months of April and October. Keeneland is the only non-profit horse racing track in the US. Another way in which this track differs from other horse racing tracks is that the 46 horse barns are open to anyone. Most other race tracks required credentials to enter the stable areas. Keeneland also stands out from other race tracks in that it has no public address system.

In addition to the main track which is a mile and a 16th long, there is also a 7-1/2 furlong turf course as well as a five-eighths mile long training track.

By the way, a furlong is an eighth of a mile

BET YOU DIDN'T KNOW...

Madisonville, seat of Hopkins County, was named for President James Madison, our fourth US President.

TRAIL OF TEARS

Every September on the weekend after Labor Day, native Americans from all over North and Central America converge on Hopkinsville for the annual "Trail of Tears" memorial. Crafts, costumes and jewelry are made and displayed while different tribes show their native dances. Here an Aztec dancer from Mexico City performs a ritualistic dance.

BET YOU DIDN'T KNOW...

Benton, seat of Marshall County, celebrates its annual "Tater Day" the first Monday each April.

There are 70 public airports in Kentucky, not including the one and only seaplane base at Kuttawa on Lake Barkley.

Sunlight and Shadows

During the fall season when the leaves turn brilliant reds and yellows, there are not very many places that can match the beauty of the Red River Gorge area. The contrast between the colorful trees in the setting sunlight across the road from the trees in the shade make an interesting picture.

Bet you didn't know...

Anderson County was formed in 1827 from parts of Franklin, Washington, and Mercer counties.

There are 110.6 people per square mile in Floyd County.

Kentucky's first industry was commercial salt production in Bullitt County.

Ringo's Mills
Covered Bridge

One of three covered bridges in Fleming County, this bridge is also closed to traffic. Built in 1867, this 86 foot long bridge spans Fox Creek. The yellow pine trusses in the top are the originals.

Bet you didn't know...

Paducah in McCracken County, was originally known as Pekin.

George Washington purchased 5,000 acres of land in Grayson County in 1788 but never lived there.

FRANKFORT IS OUR CAPITAL

Because of overcrowding and disrepair of the old capital, Governor J.W.W. Beckham promoted construction for a new one. The cost was $1,820,000 and funds for Civil and Spanish-American War claims paid for half of this. The cornerstone was laid in 1906 and was dedicated in June 1910 under Governor A.E. Willson's term. The dome and rotunda are of French influence and are designed like the tomb of Napoleon. The white marble stairs with banisters are like those found in the Paris Opera House.

As was customary, other contenders for the honor of being selected as the permanent seat of Kentucky offered their lists of contributions. Among those hoping to be selected as the Kentucky capital were Legerwood's Bend in Mercer County, Delaney's Ferry and Petersburg, both in Woodford County; Louisville, Lexington and Frankfort. After careful consideration of all sites, the commissioners, following a majority vote, met with the legislature in Lexington Dec. 5, 1792 and gave their recommendation. As you might have guessed, Frankfort was voted the most suitable site for the state capital.

NADA TUNNEL

The Nada Tunnel is an old railroad logging tunnel which is now open to cars. Eight hundred feet long, 12 feet high and 11 feet wide, can make you feel like you are being squeezed, but it is kind of neat to drive through. This is the way you want to go to drive the Red River Gorge Loop, a 36 mile scenic drive through some of the most beautiful wilderness you will ever see, especially in the fall when the leaves change color. KY 77 meets with KY 715 for this trip. The Red River Gorge contains over 150 natural sandstone arches and three waterfalls. For those who like to hike, there is a 38 mile system of loop trails.

BET YOU DIDN'T KNOW...

Fort Knox has approximately 3,800 buildings.

Bet you didn't know...

10 percent of the land in Clinton County is owned by the federal government.

Until 1996 the state tree was the Kentucky Coffee Tree, which was actually a mahogany tree. However, that year it was changed so that now the state tree is the Tulip Poplar.

CLARK COUNTY COURTHOUSE

When this picture was taken, the early morning sunrise made the courthouse in Winchester stand out like a sore thumb. This picture even appeared on the front page of the Winchester Sun whose office can be seen to the right rear of the courthouse.

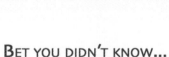

BET YOU DIDN'T KNOW...

In 1990, the number of college graduates in Kentucky over the age of 25 was 318,127. That means out of every 1,000 graduates in the US only nine of them live in Kentucky.

Allen County covers an area of 346 square miles.

PINEVILLE

From the top of the mountain, the picturesque town of Pineville in Bell County, can be seen below. It is situated alongside US 25E and the Cumberland River.

BET YOU DIDN'T KNOW...

In Shelby County, 64.6 people live in each square mile of area.

Breckenridge County has the longest county name in Kentucky.

VALLEY VIEW FERRY

Names for the location of the picturesque Valley View community in Madison County is Kentucky's oldest continuous business of record.

In 1780 John Craig acquired land through a military warrant. In 1785 the Virginia assembly granted a perpetual irrevocable franchise to establish a ferry.

BET YOU DIDN'T KNOW...

Gallatin County is Kentucky's smallest county in regards to land size at 98 square miles.

Kentucky has 13,000 miles of streams.

BATTLE OF PERRYVILLE

On Oct. 8, 1862 one of the bloodiest battles of the US Civil War took place at this site. Twelve thousand Confederate soldiers under the direction of Gen. E. Kirby Smith controlled the central part of Kentucky. At this time Gen. Braxton Bragg, commander of the Army of Tennessee was moving his troops northward to join forces with Gen. Smiths' thereby gaining control of the entire state.

The Union commander, Maj. Gen. Don Carlos Buell was headed toward Louisville to save the major Union supply base from capture. Buell managed to get there first, giving him a tactical advantage.

When the Union and Confederate forces met in battle, nearly 40,000 men were directly involved in the fighting and there were over 7,500 casualties.

Disregarding the advice of his officers to re-engage the out-numbered Union forces, Bragg retreated to Harrodsburg even though the Confederates had done very well. On the other side, Gen. Buell allowed the Confederates to withdraw unmolested which caused him to be relieved of his command.

LOUISVILLE SLUGGER

This monstrous bat stands outside the Louisville Slugger museum in downtown Louisville. It is an exact scale replica of the bat that Babe Ruth requested in the 1920s. Ruth used a model R43, which was a 34 inch bat.

This "big bat" is 120 feet tall, nine feet in diameter at the base and weights 68,000 pounds. It is made of carbon steel.

The oval "signature logo" on the bat has the name of John A. "Bud" Hillerich, who in 1884 turned the company's first bat.

BET YOU DIDN'T KNOW...

Diane Sawyer, television correspondent and journalist, was born in Glasgow, seat of Barren County.

By 1905 the Amos Buggy Co. in Owensboro, Daviess County, was the largest privately owned buggy manufacturer in the US and produced 125 buggies a day.

GOOD OL' BOYS

These good ol' boys are causing the fish to stress out in Dale Hollow Lake. If you like to kick back like these guys and fish for small mouth bass, then Dale Hollow Lake is the place to be. The world record catch for small mouth bass came out of this lake.

BET YOU DIDN'T KNOW...

World famous inventor Thomas A. Edison spent two years in Louisville as a telegrapher. He arrived in the spring of 1866 after being fired as a telegraph operator in Memphis. However, he didn't last long in Louisville either. It seems as though during an experiment, the young Edison spilled several gallons of sulfuric acid on the floor which ate through the wood and leaked down into the newly-decorated room of manager T.R. Boyle. Edison was fired the next day.

BET YOU DIDN'T KNOW...

John Taliaferro Thompson, who was born in Newport, designed the first submachine gun. It was known as the "Thompson submachine gun" or "Tommygun" and was a favorite weapon among gangsters of the prohibition era.

Lexington's Transylvania University was the first regular institution of learning founded in the West.

BET YOU DIDN'T KNOW...

In 1776, Burkesville in Cumberland County was known as Cumberland Crossing, VA. Kentucky had not yet separated from Virginia then.

Harlan was originally known as Mt. Pleasant.

JOHNSON CREEK COVERED BRIDGE

One of only 13 remaining covered bridges left in Kentucky, this bridge is located in Robertson County. Robertson County is Kentucky's second smallest county.

BET YOU DIDN'T KNOW...

Kentucky is divided into five regions: the Eastern Coalfields, Bluegrass, Pennyroyal (Pennyrile), Western Coalfields and the Jackson Purchase. Some consider the "Knobs" as a sixth region.

ABRAHAM LINCOLN'S BOYHOOD HOME

Southwest of New Haven in Larue County is the replica of the cabin where young Abraham Lincoln lived as a boy. The cabin, rebuilt in 1931, stands on the original site of the 228 acre farm known as Knob Creek. The original cabin was torn down in 1870 and until that time it had been used as a corn crib.

Abe lived on this farm from the time he was 2 until he was almost 8 years old. His baby brother was born and died here.

BET YOU DIDN'T KNOW...

Frank and Jesse James' parents were both born in Kentucky. Their father, Robert S. James of Logan County was a Georgetown College ministerial student. Their mother, Zerela (Cole) James was born in Woodford County where her grandfather operated a stagecoach inn. A picture of the Offutt-Cole Tavern is located elsewhere in this book.

OLD ONE FIFTY-TWO

Here she comes right on schedule. This is the only Louisville and Nashville steam locomotive that has been restored.

Built in 1950, it pulled passenger trains on the L&N's Lebanon Branch, which was one of the first railways built by the old L&N as they were making their way south in the 1850s. They reached Boston, KY November 1856 and had the tracks laid to New Haven by July 1857 and by later that year the tracks reached Lebanon.

Realizing the benefits that the railroad would bring, farmers who lived along the route did a lot of the work. Being a vital supply and transportation artery during the Civil War, it was often targeted by confederate soldiers.

BLESSING OF THE HOUNDS

Before the annual fox hunt at the Iroquois Hunt Club in Fayette County, a priest prays and blesses the hounds.

BET YOU DIDN'T KNOW...

Jamestown, in Russell County, used to be called Jacksonville.

Fifty-one of Kentucky's county seats are located on rivers.

THE OHIO RIVER MEETS THE MISSISSIPPI RIVER

This aerial picture shows the blue water of the Ohio draining into the muddy Mississippi River near Wickliffe, KY, seat of Ballard County. The point at which two (or more) rivers meet is called a confluence. Looking northward, Kentucky is shown at the bottom. Above the Ohio River and to the right of the Mississippi River is Illinois and the top left shows Missouri.

Can you see the tugboat maneuvering a barge in the middle of the confluence?

BET YOU DIDN'T KNOW...

Roman Catholics makeup approximately 10 percent of Kentucky's population.

WORLD'S LARGEST APPLE PIE

The Casey County Apple Festival in Liberty is the site for this apple pie billed as the "World's Largest." George Wolford, the head honcho of this pie says, "A lot of other states make pies larger than this, but theirs is not made to be edible. This one is not only edible, but it gets completely eaten almost every year." He went on to say, "If it can't be eaten, then it's not a pie and these other states that bake larger ones can't eat theirs, so we stick with our claim of having the world's largest."

This particular pie is baked in a pan that is 10 feet in diameter and is eight inches deep. The pan weights 840 pounds. The pie contains 80-90 bushels of apples, 600 pounds of pasta, 300 pounds of sugar, 150 pounds of cornstarch and 25 pounds of butter. It takes 12 hours to bake and weighs over 3,000 pounds.

Wouldn't this be good with a dump truck load of ice cream on top. Yummy!

DIXIE CUP WATER TOWER

This unusual water tower happens to be at the Dixie Cup plant in Lexington.

BET YOU DIDN'T KNOW...

The Jackson Purchase region in extreme western Kentucky was surveyed using the township method. This type of survey results in a lot of straight lines for boundaries. This is different from the rest of Kentucky which was surveyed using the "metes and bounds" method.

VIETNAM MEMORIAL

This solemn memorial was built as a place of quiet meditation and to reflect upon the nature of the Vietnam War and honor those who served. It is also used as a place of ceremony and remembrance to honor those who lost their lives in this conflict.

The Plaza, as it is known, takes the form of a large sundial whose shadow points to and touches the name of each Kentuckian killed in service of the anniversary of his death. Each hour line of the sundial represents a year of American service during the war; thus, each sector between the walkways includes on year of service in Vietnam. The length of the shadow of the gnomon (pointer) varies with the season of the year. The longest shadows at the winter solstice, December 21 and the shortest June 21, the summer solstice.

It is designed so that each Kentuckian killed is honored with a personal memorial day since the tip of the gnomon shadow touches that name on the anniversary of death. The names of those missing in action or prisoners of war are located behind the gnomon where the shadow will never fall.

Bet you didn't know...

Elkton, county seat of Todd County, has no traffic lights.

The geographic center of Kentucky is outside of Lebanon in Marion County. It is located on private property which is being used as a dairy farm.

READY FOR THE CHASE

These members of the Iroquois Hunt Club ride along Grimes Mill Road as they near the field where the actual fox hunt begins. The fox hunt is an annual event held every November in Fayette County.

BET YOU DIDN'T KNOW...

When Abraham Lincoln was born near Hodgensville, it was in Hardin County. Hodgensville is now in LaRue County which became a county in 1843.

BET YOU DIDN'T KNOW...

Paris was originally named Hopewell.

There are three national monuments in Kentucky: the Lincoln Birthplace, Cumberland Gap and Mammoth Cave.

Loretta Lynn's Childhood Home

This cabin home sits in a part of Johnson County known as Butcher Hollow. It is where Loretta Webb, better known as country singer Loretta Lynn grew up. This home was made famous by her song titled Coalminers Daughter.

Bet you didn't know...

Kentucky ranks 25th in population. The 2000 census shows the population to be 4,041,769.

There are 17 Kentucky governors buried in the Frankfort Cemetery.

DOVER COVERED BRIDGE

This is one of two covered bridges located in Mason County, the other being the Valley Pike Covered Bridge.

BET YOU DIDN'T KNOW...

Stanford, in Lincoln County, is the second oldest permanent settlement in Kentucky.

The average yearly temperature for Kentucky is 55 degrees Fahrenheit.

MY OLD KENTUCKY HOME

This mansion is in Bardstown in Nelson County and sits on 285 acres better known as Federal Hill. It was built in 1818 by Judge John Rowan, who served in both the US Senate and the Kentucky Court of Appeals.

Stephen Foster, visiting his cousin here in 1852, got the inspiration to write My Old Kentucky Home, which became the official name of this Kentucky landmark.

BET YOU DIDN'T KNOW...

Carlisle, in Nicholas County is the site of Daniel Boone's last home in Kentucky.

THE OLD "SHED HOUSE"

All right! All right! Know what you are thinking. "What a great place to put his book to some good use."

ELK COW

Elk are rather shy animals and it is kind of difficult to get close to them but this young cow held a pose. This particular elk is at the Elk Bison Prairie at Land Between the Lakes. To get a picture of these animals, go late in the afternoon just before sundown when they come out of the brush and head for the watering hole.

Elk are members of the deer family, but males and females are known as bulls and cows, not bucks and does.

BET YOU DIDN'T KNOW...

Kentucky's first newspaper was the *Kentucky Gazette*, founded in Lexington in 1787.

CAPITAL ON THE RIVER

This aerial view shows the state capital at Frankfort and its proximity to the Kentucky River. Looking real close, you can see the floral clock to the right rear of the capital building.

BET YOU DIDN'T KNOW...

Forests still cover more than two-fifths of the state's land area or about 17,200 square miles.

One-quarter of Edmonson County is in Mammoth Cave National Park.

TINY CHAPEL

This tiny chapel is along a country roadside in Wayne County near the town of Monticello. It is open to the public and has enough benches or pews to seat about five or six people. It also has a pulpit. The picnic table beside it will seat as many people as the chapel.

BET YOU DIDN'T KNOW...

The Union Soldier Monument in Vanceburg is the only one of its kind south of the Mason-Dixon line.

Kentucky has 679 square miles of inland water.

DALE HOLLOW LAKE

Sitting on the Kentucky-Tennessee border, this lake covers 27,000 acres. Dale Hollow is the site of the world record catch or small mouth bass at 11 pounds, 15 ounces. The state park here has the largest concentration of deer in Kentucky.

BET YOU DIDN'T KNOW...

Kentucky is the top producer of bourbon whiskey in the US.

Webster County is bordered on the east by the Green River while the Tradewater River forms the western border.

OLD PROVIDENCE CHURCH

Located in southern Clark County close to the Kentucky River stands this church where Daniel Boone attended. Squire, Jr., Samuel and Mary Boone were baptized here.

Originally known as Howard's Creek Church, the name was changed in 1790 to Providence. William Bush, a member of Boone's second Kentucky expedition, built the present stone structure of native limestone. United Baptists formed here in 1801. The church was restored after slight fire damage in 1949.

BET YOU DIDN'T KNOW...

The eastern coal fields provide three-fourths of Kentucky's bituminous (soft) coal. The coal mined in the western coal fields is of a lower quality due to a higher concentration of sulfur and ash content.

INSIDE CARTER CAVE

Dripping water creates some very unusual formations inside of Carter Cave. This cave system is made up of over 20 caverns.

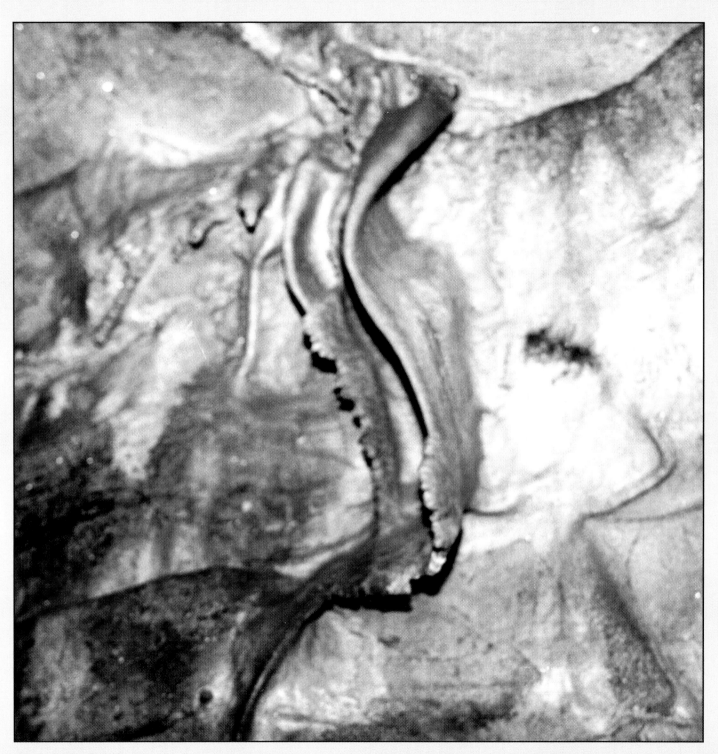

BET YOU DIDN'T KNOW...

Henderson, sitting on the banks of the Ohio River was once the tobacco capital of the US since the river provided access to world-wide shipping. Henderson used to be the richest town per capita in the US.

POULTRY POETRY

On a bench behind the courthouse
He sat in bibbed overalls,
Chewing on a plug of tobacco
The grass brown, where his spit
falls.

I sat down on a neighboring bench
As he gave me the once-over look,
He turned his head to spit tobacco
I pulled out my favorite book.

I guess he was starved for small-talk
and said, "What kinda bid'ness
you in?",
I told him my business was poetry
"Po'try!" he said with a grin.

"I used to be in that bid'ness myself"
He said as we started to chat,
I told him I'd like to hear about it
As he adjusted his tattered ball cap.

"I wuz in the po'try bid'ness for 40
years"
He took another spit and then,
"5,000 of 'em I ended up with"
"Started out with one rooster and
one hen!"

FRANKLIN COUNTY

No historical significance, just a pretty picture.

BET YOU DIDN'T KNOW...

The original log courthouse in Somerset, Pulaski County seat, cost $23 to build in 1801.

Tomkinsville, county seat of Monroe County was originally called Watson's Store.

NOT MUCH OF A CROP THIS YEAR

This single tobacco plant looks kind of lonely on this farm in Clark County. Behind it is a corn field. And speaking of corn...

CABIN CREEK
COVERED BRIDGE

This Lewis County covered bridge is no longer open to traffic. A more modern paved road now crosses Cabin Creek right next to the old covered bridge.

BET YOU DIDN'T KNOW...

The Southern Bank of Russellville was robbed of $9,000 in 1868 by Jesse James and his gang.

The state flower of Kentucky is the goldenrod.

Balloons In Berea

Berea is nestled in southern Madison County and was the location for the start of a hot air balloon race during the annual Spoonbread Festival.

In 1850 this area was known as the Glade and was mostly comprised of farms and a racetrack.

In 1853, a free tract of land was given to Reverend John G. Fee by an ambitious politician named Cassius M. Clay. Reverend Fee, local supporters and other abolitionist missionaries from the American Missionary Assn. established a church, Berea College and a tiny village which was named Berea, after a biblical town where the people "received the Word with all readiness of mind."

Bet you didn't know...

The Kentucky River creates the border for many counties but only completely dissects two counties, Franklin and Carroll.

THE SQUIRREL HUNTER

The whittler was sitting on the porch
Telling stories of mountain folklore
This story he told of a walnut on a
    stump
About 10 feet from the shore.

A squirrel saw the nut but couldn't
    figure out
How to get the nut from the stump
But after several minutes of wanting
    that nut
He finally got the nerve to jump.

He landed on the stump and ate the
    nut
Then I guess it occurred to him
How would he get back to the shore
'Cause this poor old squirrel couldn't
    swim.

As he sat on the stump trying to figure
    it out
The water began to churn
And out of the water jumped a big old
    muskie
And a meal of squirrel he did earn.

A few minutes later that muskie came
    back
In his jaw there was a lump
As he leaped in the air he was seen to
    spit
Another walnut down onto that
    stump!

Do you Know What This Is?

Probably not, if you are not a pilot. The transmitter in this building is known as a VOR, which stand for Very High Frequency Omnidirectional Range. It is a navigation aid that pilots use to find their way through the skies and are located all over the US. By turning in to specific frequencies, a pilot an fly "to" or "from" a VOR. The VOR here in Lexington is identified by the letters HYK.

Bet you didn't know...

The Battle of Perryville was the most important Civil War engagement fought in Kentucky.

Happy Birthday to You, the world's most frequently sung song, after national anthems, was written by two Louisville sisters, Mildred and Patricia Hill.

NATURAL BRIDGE

Kentucky has a lot of "natural bridges" but this one is the most famous. It is a sandstone arch that has been formed by the forces of rain, wind and erosion for millions of years. Natural Bridge is not the largest or the oldest natural arch in the Red River Gorge area, but it is what most people come to see. This became a tourist attraction in the 19th century.

BET YOU DIDN'T KNOW...

Twenty-six states have mountain peaks higher than Kentucky's Black Mountain, which is the highest point in the state at 4,145 feet above sea level.

YAHOO FALLS

The tallest waterfall in Kentucky is here in McCreary County. This waterfall drops 113 feet. Though not as spectacular as Cumberland Falls, this is well worth seeing if you like waterfalls, especially after the heavy spring rains.

BET YOU DIDN'T KNOW...

The curved part of Kentucky just southeast of the confluence where the Ohio River meets the Mississippi River is known as the "Monkey's Eyebrow" because of its shape. There is also a small community of the same name located near there.

FIRST POST OFFICE

Built a little before 1792, this is the original building that served as the first post office west of the Alleghenies. Thomas Barbee was commissioned as the first postmaster Aug. 20, 1792. The first mail was received here Nov. 3, 1792. This building is located in Constitution Square in Danville.

BET YOU DIDN'T KNOW...

The only town in Kentucky named for a Native American is Paducah, county seat of McCracken County. It was named for the legendary Chickasaw leader, Chief Paduke.

The original name of Maysville was Limestone Landing.

KENTUCKY STATE PENITENTIARY

Located in Eddyville in Lyon County this is the only maximum security facility in Kentucky. There are also nine medium security, two minimum security and three private prisons in Kentucky.

Kentucky State Penitentiary (KSP) has an average daily population of 828 inmates. The cost of incarcerating one inmate at KSP is $49.25 per day, or $18,025.57 per year.

Originally known as Kentucky Branch Penitentiary, the facility was opened for business on Christmas Eve 1890 after six years of construction and $420,000.

In 1906 the first prisoner was sent here for execution and in 1912 the facility was renamed Kentucky State Penitentiary.

During the period 1928-29 49 men were executed here and in 1929 seven men were electrocuted in one night, which is still the national record for the most electrocuted in one day. To date, executions have been 51 percent white and 49 percent black.

In March 1998, the Execution Law in Kentucky was changed to lethal injection.

CHAINED ROCK

On the mountain top above Pineville, seat of Bell County, is what is known as "Chained Rock." As superstition tells it, the chain is supposed to prevent the large rock from tumbling down the mountain into the town.

The two cuties in the picture are the author's twin daughters. He says "Aw, c'mon folks, give me a break! I had to put them in the book somewhere. After all, they are my youngin's."

BET YOU DIDN'T KNOW...

Kentucky is 458 miles wide east to west and 171 miles north to south.

Grant County covers 259 square miles.

RED RIVER GORGE

The fall season is the favorite time to pack a lunch and camera and go hiking down this trail.

BET YOU DIDN'T KNOW...

Six Kentucky counties are named for US presidents: Jefferson, Madison, Washington, Harrison, Monroe and Taylor. Sorry about that Lincoln, Clinton, Johnson, Jackson, Grant and Carter counties. Their names are not associated with presidents.

FLORENCE Y'ALL

This water tower in Boone County tells travelers on I-75 where they are the southern way.

BET YOU DIDN'T KNOW...

After witnessing a slave auction on the courthouse lawn in Washington, KY Harriet Beecher Stowe got the idea to write *Uncle Tom's Cabin*.

In the television miniseries *Centennial*, the setting was supposed to be 19th century St. Louis, but was really Augusta, KY.

Switzer Covered Bridge

This bridge spans the North Fork of the Elkhorn Creek outside of Frankfort. Sadly, just a short while after this picture was taken, a flood washed the bridge away from its foundations. It is being rebuilt, but glad to have a picture of the old bridge.

Including the Switzer Covered Bridge, there are 13 covered bridges in Kentucky. The Colville Covered Bridge is in Bourbon County near Paris; Mt. Zion Covered Bridge is in Washington County near Springfield; Bennett's Mill Bridge and Oldtown Bridge are both in Greenup County; Cabin Creek Bridge is in Lewis County near Maysville; Dover Bridge and Valley Pike Bridge are both located in Mason County near Maysville; Fleming County has three covered bridges: Goddard Bridge, Hillsboro Bridge and Ringo's Mill Bridge; Johnson Creek Bridge is in Robertson County near Blue Licks Battlefield State Park and Bracken County has Walcott Bridge.

THE MILL AT MILL SPRINGS

This Wayne County mill still works and grinds cornmeal every Saturday. The waterpowered wheel is 40 feet in diameter and is fed by 13 natural springs that are located beside the mill. The mill was first built in 1818 and later served as a fortification for Confederate troops during the Civil War. In 1877 a miller erected the present mill.

The mill is on Mill Springs Park which was also the site for one of the greatest Civil War battles ever. On Jan. 19, 1862 Union and Confederate forces clashed here where 125 Confederate soldiers died, including their commander, Gen. Felix K. Zollicoffer. It was the first major defeat for Confederate forces since the breakout of the Civil War. With the Union finally getting a victory under their belt this battle began a string of setbacks for the Confederacy which eventually allowed Union troops to move through Kentucky and into Tennessee.

Cumberland Gap Tunnel

Located on US 25E this tunnel is an engineering marvel. It all began on June 21, 1991 when the first rock was blasted. Appalachian coal miners and construction workers were joined by workers from Austria, Italy, Germany, Canada, France and China.

The tunnel is actually twin tunnels that are 4,600 feet in length and 30 feet high at the highest point. There are cross passages every 300 feet which connect the two tunnels and provide fire extinguishers and telephones for emergency use.

Both tunnels are lined with thick PVC material to make sure that the tunnels stay dry.

Operators are on duty 24 hours a day, seven days a week. Ambulances, fire-rescue trucks and wreckers are located at each portal building. In order to respond to any emergency, all operators at the tunnel are cross-trained as firefighters and emergency medical technicians.

The tunnel took 1,947 days to complete and was opened to the public Oct. 18, 1996.

BISON

Bison originally came to North America from Asia. More commonly known as buffalo, the bison is the largest land animal in North America standing 6-1/2 feet high at the shoulder hump. A mature bull can be from nine to 12 feet long and can weigh from 1800 to 2400 pounds. "Told you there would be a lot of bull in this book!" The bison deserves to be our national emblem rather than the eagle. The bison fed and clothed our Native Americans. Its hide was also used to make teepees to provide shelter. Even dried buffalo dung was burned to keep warm and for cooking. These majestic creatures were almost slaughtered to extinction in the late 1800s for no other reason than to drive the Indians from their lands.

BET YOU DIDN'T KNOW...

So far there have been 358 miles of cave passages explored in Mammoth Cave National Park.

SUNRISE OVER TUSCALOOSA LANE

The homes in this quiet residential neighborhood in Lexington cast beautiful shadows as the sun begins to peek over the horizon.

BET YOU DIDN'T KNOW...

Breaks Interstate Park, near Elkhorn City is known as the "Grand Canyon of the East" and is the largest canyon east of the Mississippi River.

Eastern Kentucky University in Richmond sits on 325 acres.

ANOTHER VIEW OF CUMBERLAND FALLS

Whew! The author huffed and puffed his way up the mountain on the other side of the falls just to give you this picture. This is what the falls look like from the McCreary County side. It looks a lot different when you can see the river before it drops off the escarpment.

BET YOU DIDN'T KNOW...

Although North Carolina is the nation's leading tobacco producing state, Kentucky is number one in the US when it comes to burley tobacco. The world's largest burley tobacco market is in Lexington.

RED RIVER IRON WORKS

There are a lot of iron furnaces found around Kentucky but this one is the largest and best preserved. Known locally in Estill County as the Fitchburg Furnace, this single stone structure is 60 feet high and is 40 feet by 60 feet. The Blackstone and Chandler twin stacks are 50 feet high and 12-1/2 feet across on the inside. Built in 1869, it operated with steam-powered air blasts, burning charcoal. It was in operation until 1874. During the 15 years of operation, it produced 16,072 tons of iron. The community of Fitchburg, chartered in 1871, no longer exists.

As a major producer since 1791, Kentucky ranked third in the US in the 1830s and was 11th by 1965. Charcoal, timber, native ore and limestone supplied material for numerous furnaces making pig iron, utensils and munitions. The old charcoal furnaces era ended by depletion of ore and timber and the growth of railroads.

By the way, in case you were wondering, pig iron is crude iron that has been cast in blocks.

Lee County Oil Well

Don't see too many of these old oil wells anymore. There are still a few left in Lee County around Beattyville.

Bet you didn't know...

In 1980 only three Kentucky counties did not grow tobacco: Letcher, Harlan and Pike.

The Kentucky-Tennessee border is known as the "Walker Line" and was named for Dr. Thomas Walker who surveyed the boundary. The border was intended to be a straight line, but because of human error, the boundary drops out of alignment near the Land Between the Lakes area in western Kentucky.

CANDLE-MAKING AT FORT BOONESBOROUGH

The shops inside Fort Boonesborough by the Kentucky River in Madison County have many "pioneer" craftsman making things as the early settlers of the original fort used to make. Candles are not made by pouring wax into a mold, but are made by dipping the weighted wick into the wax, pulling it out, letting it cool and dipping it again. Each time the candle is dipped more wax sticks to it until the candle has reached its desired size.

Candles of many different colors are made here and several are usually made at a time.

A person who makes candles is known as a chandler.

BET YOU DIDN'T KNOW...

There are 72,632 miles of road in Kentucky; 761 of these miles comprise the states interstate highways.

Bet you didn't know...

Henry County was named for Patrick Henry who was famous for saying, "Give me liberty or give me death."

In Livingston County, the elevation ranges from 302 feet to 754 feet above sea level.

The Owsley County seat, now known as Booneville, was once known as Boone's Station because Daniel Boone once camped near there.

Clark County covers 259 square miles, or 165,760 acres.

The world's two largest mules, documented by the *Guiness Book of World Records* were on a farm in Bullitt County. They have since died.

PENN'S PRIVY

What have you always wanted to know about outhouses? Have you ever wondered why there is a crescent moon on the doors? This is because outhouses were around before electricity and in order to let in light during the nighttime hours, a hole was cut in the door above the line of sight for privacy and to let in moonlight. It was not a good idea to take a lantern into the outhouse at night because an explosion could result from the open flame. Fact is, most people kept a covered pot under the bed for night use. Another reason for the crescent moon is that the ancient symbol for the moon, Luna, represents womanhood. One theory claims that the crescent moon was carved into the door to signify the ladies facilities and the symbol for man, Sol, the sun, was represented by a round hole. Men's facilities were not usually kept in as good condition as the ladies and most men's deteriorated. The ladies outhouses lasted longer and the crescent moon remained the sybmol.

Most outhouses had two holes in the seat. A smaller one for children and a larger one for adults. Children quickly learned which one NOT to sit on.

The standard outhouse stands 6'6" at the front and 5'6" at the rear. The roof width is 5'8". From front to back, the length of the roof was 6'. The floor diminsions were usually 4'X4'. The pit should be dug 3'6" square and 4'11" deep.

BENNETT'S MILL
COVERED BRIDGE

This is one of two covered bridges in Greenup County, the other being the Oldtown Bridge. Bennett's Mill Bridge was built over Tygart's Creek in 1855 and is one of the longest one-span covered bridges in Kentucky. You can still drive over this 195 foot bridge.

BET YOU DIDN'T KNOW...

Morehead became the seat of Rowan County in 1856 when the county was formed. Prior to that, the post office there was known as Triplett.

Mark Twains' mother was born in Adair County.

Kentucky had a county named Beckham, but it was only in existence for 60 days. Olive Hill was the county seat.

WEIGHT LIMIT 3 TONS

OLD TALBOTT TAVERN

The author is glad to have gotten a picture of the Old Talbott Tavern before it burned. It is the oldest inn west of the Allegheny Mountains. In addition to that, it is the oldest western stagecoach stop in America since 1779. This famous landmark is located in Bardstown which is known for many more interesting sites. Among them are My Old Kentucky Home on Federal Hill where Stephen Foster wrote the famous ballad of the same name. Bardstown is also known as the "Bourbon Capital of the World," had the oldest operating jail in the state until 1987 and was the site of the original Court of Appeals.

BET YOU DIDN'T KNOW...

J.C.W. Beckham was Kentucky's youngest governor at 30 years and five months.

The Shawnee Indian word for elk is "wapiti" which means white rump.

BET YOU DIDN'T KNOW...

Most elk calves are born in June.

The Duncan Tavern in Paris was the first tavern in Kentucky to sell bourbon. Both Daniel Boone and Simon Kenton used to stop in here for refreshments.

Former President and Mrs. George Bush had a dog in the White House named "Millie" that was bred in Midway.

Salyersville, seat of Magoffin County used to be known as Adamsville.

Fog on the Kentucky River

The morning fog follows the Kentucky River along the boundary between Clark and Madison counties.

Bet you didn't know...

Whitesburg was the home of Franklin Gary Powers, the pilot of the U2 spy plane that was shot down over the Soviet Union during the Eisenhower administration.

Fort Knox is situated on 109,000 acres and is in three different counties: Meade, Hardin and Bullitt.

MAYSVILLE FROM THE HILLTOP

From the top of the hill a beautiful view of part of downtown Maysville can be seen. The focal point of this picture is the Simon Kenton Bridge spanning the Ohio River. Although smaller, this bridge is an exact replica of San Francisco's famed Golden Gate Bridge.

BET YOU DIDN'T KNOW...

Kentucky's other US Army military reservation is Fort Campbell, which is in parts of Trigg and Christian counties and the Tennessee counties of Stewart and Montgomery. The base covers 101,755 acres.

The Scott County courthouse is the county's fourth and was completed in 1877.

WORLD'S LARGEST FLOATING FOUNTAIN

The Louisville Falls Fountain is the largest floating fountain in the world. Near the dam on the Ohio River, 42 jets spray 15,800 gallons of water per minute up to 400 feet into the air. Due to disrepair, the fountain is currently no longer in the river.

BET YOU DIDN'T KNOW...

Warren County is located in both the Pennyrile and Western Coalfield regions.

Mount Vernon, seat of Rockcastle County, was originally called White Rock.

JEFFERSON DAVIS MONUMENT

In the Todd County community of Fairview, construction of the world's tallest obelisk began in 1917 on this 19 acre site. By 1918 the monument had reached a height of 175 feet but construction had to be halted because of rationing of building materials during WWI.

In January 1922 construction resumed and the monument was completed in 1924 at an increased cost of $200,000 over the original estimate of $75,000. The completed monument stands 351 feet tall and rests on a foundation of solid Kentucky limestone. The walls are seven feet thick at the base and taper to two feet thick where the point inclines.

Jefferson Davis was the only president of the Confederate States of America during the Civil War. He also founded The Army Medical Corps, suggested that a transcontinental railroad connect the Atlantic with the Pacific Oceans and wrote the Rise and Fall of the Confederate Government.

BET YOU DIDN'T KNOW...

An obelisk is a four-sided pillar with sloping sides ending with a pyramid on top.

BET YOU DIDN'T KNOW...

The oldest surviving courthouse in Kentucky is in Greensburg, seat of Green County. Built in 1802, it was in use until 1931.

BET YOU DIDN'T KNOW...

The area of Kentucky is 40,395 square miles.

During the period 1920-33 the town of Golden Pond, in western Kentucky's Land Between the Lakes area, was known as the "moonshine capital of the world."

Bet you didn't know...

The town of Henderson, in Henderson County was originally known as Red Banks.

The state flag of Kentucky was designed by Frankfort art teacher Jessie Cox according to specifications of a General Assembly act of March 26, 1918.

GRAY'S ARCH

Located in the beautiful Red River Gorge area, this natural sandstone arch is actually larger than Natural Bridge. A lot of people don't know about this because it takes a little more effort to get to this one since you have to hike to get here.

BET YOU DIDN'T KNOW...

Catlettsburg, seat of Boyd County, used to be known as Mouth of Sandy.

When Abraham Lincoln was a boy, his father Thomas, was a carpenter in the Elizabethtown area.

OLDTOWN COVERED BRIDGE

This is the "new" Oldtown Covered Bridge the day after it was dedicated. The author wanted to get a picture of it before it got covered with graffiti. This bridge is one of two covered bridges located in Greenup County.

Originally built in 1880, this two-span bridge is 194 feet long and is over the Little Sandy River.

BET YOU DIDN'T KNOW...

Wilmore used to be known as Scott's Station.

There are seven major streams in Kentucky: The Tennessee, Cumberland, Tradewater, Green, Salt, Kentucky and Licking rivers.

ABRAHAM LINCOLN BIRTHPLACE

In 1909, almost 100 years after Abraham Lincoln was born on this farmland, President Theodore Roosevelt laid the cornerstone for this memorial. Two years later in 1911 the shrine was dedicated by President William Howard Taft.

The Lincoln birthplace cabin is located inside the marble and granite structure but there is some doubt as to whether or not it is the actual cabin that Lincoln was born in.

There are 56 steps leading up to the entrance, one step for each year of Lincoln's life.

BET YOU DIDN'T KNOW...

Kentucky's Abraham Lincoln has been the tallest President of the US thus far, standing six feet, four inches tall.

Winchester

Depot Street is one of the few streets left that is still paved with bricks. Winchester is the seat of Clark County and is the author's hometown.

Bet you didn't know...

The reason that Kentucky has no large, natural lakes is because during the last Ice Age, about 10,000 years ago, the glaciers did not get down this far. The leading edge of the glaciers stopped around what is now the Ohio River. Land that has been covered by glaciers is flatter than land that has not been covered. The immense weight of the glaciers also cause large depressions in the soft earth which fill with water as the glaciers recede, creating lakes.

BULL ELK

This bull displays a rather impressive rack. Wish he would have been facing forward, but animal pictures are tough since they won't always do what you want them to.

In late winter, he will shed his antlers and start growing new ones in early spring.

BET YOU DIDN'T KNOW...

That part of the Daniel Boone National Forest located in Kentucky covers 687,000 acres in 21 counties. The forest has 500 miles of trails and 800 miles of roads.

High Bridge

Located in Wilmore in Jessamine County, High Bridge was the first cantilever bridge built on the American continent. It was the most remarkable bridge in the US when constructed in 1876. The bridge was replaced in 1911 using the same foundations without stopping rail service.

When construction was completed High Bridge was the highest railroad bridge in the US over a navigable stream (308 feet). It was planned as a suspension bridge for the Lexington and Danville Railroad by John Roebling who was the designer of the famous Brooklyn Bridge in New York City. The huge stone towers to hold the cables were built in 1851 but work on the bridge was abandoned during the Civil War. The stone towers were removed in 1929 by the Southern Railroad to permit double tracks.

This aerial picture was taken just as a train was passing over the bridge and the Dixie Belle riverboat was getting ready to pass under it.

Falmouth, seat of Pendleton County was originally known as Forks of Licking.

Robertson County is the least populated county in Kentucky.

KENTUCKY DAM

Located near Gilbertsville, the longest dam in Kentucky. Completed in 1944, it stands 208 feet high and is 8,422 feet wide. It took six years to build, required 5,000 workers, 1.3 million cubic yards of concrete, 5.5 million cubic yards of earth and rockfill and cost $118 million.

This dam, built across the Tennessee River, created Kentucky Lake which is the largest lake in the TVA (Tennessee Valley Authority) system. The lake extends from within 20 miles of the Illinois state line, all the way through Kentucky and into Tennessee. It is 184 miles long and is between 1-1/4 and 2-1/2 miles wide. Kentucky Lake has over 2,380 miles of shoreline. The surface area covers over 160,000 acres.

BET YOU DIDN'T KNOW...

The highest point in Kentucky is Black Mountain in Harlan County and stands 4,145 feet above sea level.

OLD FORT HARROD

On June 16, 1774 a town was laid out and named Harrodstown by Capt. James Harrod. He and 32 men had left Pennsylvania earlier that year to claim lands and settle a community.

The graves of 500 pioneers are contained in the pioneer cemetery, which is the oldest cemetery west of the Allegheny Mountains.

The cabin where Abraham Lincoln's parents were married was moved here from its original location near Springfield. A brick building now shelters the cabin.

BET YOU DIDN'T KNOW...

The three original counties in Kentucky were Fayette, Jefferson and Lincoln.

Todd County was named for Col. John Todd who was the great uncle of Mary Todd Lincoln, Abe's wife.

THE RED MILE

Harness racing began at this 175 acre complex Sept. 28, 1975. A bay colt named Odd Fellow won the first race run here, the Lexington Stakes.

In 1892 the one mile track was moved to its present location in Fayette County and a half mile track was added to the infield.

There are two types of harness racing horses, trotters and pacers. Trotters move a front foot and the opposite rear foot at the same time while pacers move both feet on the same side of the body simultaneously.

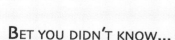

BET YOU DIDN'T KNOW...

Union County has bragging rights when it comes to who is the top corn producer in Kentucky.

Kentucky is spread over 25,500,000 acres.

Kentucky ranks 37th in size among the 50 states.

Ohio calls itself the Buckeye State but the largest buckeye tree in the US is in Casey County, KY. It is 12 feet, seven inches in circumference, four feet in diameter at the base, has 135 branches and stands 148 feet tall.

BET YOU DIDN'T KNOW...

Lee County is the only Kentucky county named for a Civil War hero. It was named for Gen. Robert E. Lee, CSA.

Beattyville was originally known as "Three Forks."

BET YOU DIDN'T KNOW...

Kentucky's 18th governor, John L. Helm (1850-51) was a member of the Whig Party. He later became the 24th governor (1867) and was a democrat.

The first four-lane highway built in Kentucky was between Frankfort and Versailles.

HILLSBORO COVERED BRIDGE

One of three covered bridges in Fleming County, this bridge was built around 1865-70 and is a single span 86 feet long.

BET YOU DIDN'T KNOW...

Only 43 counties in Kentucky allow (legal) sales of alcohol.

Georgia and Texas are the only states that have more counties than Kentucky.

OLD STATE HOUSE IN FRANKFORT

During the period 1827-1829, Kentucky's third capital was built on this site. The two previous capitals were destroyed by fire.

This old capital was built of Kentucky River marble and the most outstanding feature is the self-supporting stone circular stairway. To expedite construction, Joel Scott, keeper of penitentiary, invented a wire saw to cut the rough stone.

This building was designed by architect Gideon Shryock of Lexington and it served as the seat of government for 80 years until completion of the new capital in 1909.

Daniel Boone and his wife, Rebecca, lay in state here in 1845 before their interment in the Frankfort Cemetery.

This was the only capital in the US to be captured by Confederate forces which took place November 1862.

Governor William Goebel was assassinated in this building Jan. 30, 1900.

Rabbit Hash
General Store

Nestled alongside the Ohio River, this little village has had a store since 1831, although the present store was built in 1919.

BET YOU DIDN'T KNOW...

Lake Barkley was created by building
Barkley Dam across the Cumberland
River. The dam, built in 1966 is 157
feet high and is 10,180 feet wide.
Lake Barkley is Kentucky's second
largest lake and covers 58,000 acres.

Fort Boonesborough

Sitting alongside the Kentucky River at the Clark-Madison County border, this is an authentic reproduction of old Fort Boone as it looked in the 1770s. There are craftsmen and women working here in the traditional dress of that time. The fort was rebuilt from the original site because of yearly flooding.

Bet you didn't know...

Bardstown was originally known as Salem.

Nelson County was formed in 1784 and was named for Virginia Governor Thomas Nelson.

IT MUST BE OCTOBER

You know it must be cool, fall, color-changing leaf, October days when the pumpkins get lined up or stacked everywhere you look. Bet a lot of these pumpkins will get carved up for Halloween jack-o-lanterns or made into delicious pumpkin pies.

BET YOU DIDN'T KNOW...

Famed frontiersman and soldier Christopher "Kit" Carson was born at Million, KY Dec. 24, 1809. Million is four miles northwest of Richmond in what is now Madison County.

BROKE LEG FALLS

Cascading off the escarpment of Broke Leg Creek, this Menifee County waterfall is approximately one hundred feet tall. It's really too bad that this state-maintained site is closed and no longer maintained by anyone. Fallen trees and debris litter the once-paved driveway to the viewing area, ditches have been dug between the road and the driveway eliminating any safe access by automobile and there is no place for parking. All that remains of the bridge spanning Broke Leg Creek right above the falls is nothing more than steel I-beams that you must carefully balance on when crossing above the falls. These falls are beautiful and should be maintained for everyone to enjoy.

BET YOU DIDN'T KNOW...

Carter County is former home of country singer/storyteller Tom T. Hall.

OLDEST MOONSHINE STILL

John W. Bailey and his family of Logan County operated this moonshine still starting in 1779. It is now located in Bullitt County and is believed to be the oldest moonshine still in America and thought to be seven years older than the still in the Smithsonian Institute in Washington, DC.

Approximately 80 percent of the whiskey produced in the US is made right here in Kentucky. In order for whiskey to be called bourbon, it must be at least 51 percent corn and aged in new charred oak barrels for at least two years. The barrels are never reused for making bourbon. The used barrels are shipped usually out-of-state for aging other whiskey products.

BET YOU DIDN'T KNOW...

There are 120 counties in Kentucky, each county has a county seat, each county seat has a courthouse, BUT there are 122 courthouses. Do you know where the extra two are?

Bet you didn't know...

Names of towns and counties of the same name can be confusing. Here are some examples: Carlisle County seat is Bardwell, but Carlisle is the county seat of Nicholas County; Jackson County seat is McKee, but Jackson is the county seat of Breathitt County; Grayson County seat is Leitchfield, but Grayson is the county seat of Carter County; Marion County seat is Lebanon, but Marion is the county seat of Crittenden County; Hickman County seat is Clinton, but Hickman is the county seat of Fulton County; Clinton County seat is Albany, but Clinton is the county seat of Hickman County; Franklin County seat is Frankfort, but Franklin is the county seat of Simpson County.

The easternmost and largest county in Kentucky is Pike County.

Munfordville, seat of Hart County, used to be known as Big Buffalo Crossing.

BET YOU DIDN'T KNOW...

Brooksville, seat of Bracken County, was originally known as Woodward's Crossroads.

Calhoun, seat of McLean County was spelled Calhoon for many years after it was incorporated in 1852.

NATURAL BRIDGE FROM THE OTHER SIDE

There are not very many different ways to photograph Natural Bridge. It has been photographed from the air but it does not look that impressive looking down on it. This natural sandstone arch is 78 feet long and 65 feet high.

The Powell-Wolfe County lines runs right through the middle of Natural Bridge so that half of it lies in each county, however, the entire Natural Bridge State Park is located in Powell County.

BET YOU DIDN'T KNOW...

Gravel Switch, in Marion County, used to be known as Prairie City.

GODDARD "WHITE" COVERED BRIDGE

On this Fleming County bridge, you can drive across Sand Lick Creek. This 63 foot long bridge is Kentucky's only surviving example of the Ithiel Town Lattice design. The bridge is held together with wooden pegs.

BET YOU DIDN'T KNOW...

Kentucky has two communities named Fairview. One is in Christian County, where you will find the Jefferson Davis Monument and the other is along US 68 in Fleming County.

BELLE OF LOUISVILLE

Originally named the Idlewild, this paddle wheel was built in Pittsburgh in 1914 and carried people and cargo in Memphis, TN. It served as a floating USO nightclub during WWII.

In 1948, under new ownership, the name was changed to the Avalon. It was during this time that she traveled from town to town for business. Ships that did this were known as "tramps."

In 1962, designated to be torn apart for scrap, Jefferson County purchased her for $34,000. Once again, the name was changed to the present Belle of Louisville and after some restoration, she embarked on her first public cruise in 1963.

The Belle of Louisville is the oldest stern wheel steamboat on the entire Mississippi River system.

BET YOU DIDN'T KNOW...

Fort Estill was located near what is now Richmond in Madison County.

US Bullion Depository

Located at Fort Knox, this gold depository was opened January 1937. Costing $560,000 this structure is 105 feet by 121 feet and stands 42 feet high. It is constructed of 16,500 cubic feet of granite, 4,200 cubic yards of concrete, 750 tons of reinforcing steel and 670 tons of structural steel. It is actually two buildings under one roof. The vault doors weigh 30 tons each.

The bullion stored here is in the form of gold bars which are seven inches by 3-5/8 by 1-3/4 inches and weigh 27-1/2 pounds each. This is equivalent to 400 troy ounces for each gold bar.

Stored here for safekeeping during WWII, were the British Magna Carta of 1215, St. Blasius-St. Paul copy of the Gutenberg Bible from 1450-55, the original Declaration of Independence, the Articles of Confederation, the original signed copy of the Constitution of the US of 1787, the original autographed copy of Abraham Lincoln's Gettysburg Address of 1863 and the original autographed copy of Lincoln's second inaugural address of 1865.

MULE POWERED CANE MILL

This is how to grind the cane the old-fashioned way to make sorghum molasses. This mill was at the Sorghum Festival in Morgan County in West Liberty.

BET YOU DIDN'T KNOW...

In Letcher County, Martin Van Buren Bates was known as "the giant of Letcher County." Born in Whitesburg, he grew to be 7 feet, 11-1/2 inches tall and weighed 478 pounds.

To provide grazing land for buffalo, the Indians burned most of the original forests creating a "barren" land. This is how Barren County got its name.

MOUNT STERLING COURT DAY

On the third weekend in October each year, the town of Mount Sterling in Montgomery County draws a crowd of an estimated 80,000-100,000 people to its annual Court Days Festival. You can buy, sell or trade anything from clothes to guns to hound dogs and just about anything else you are looking for. This aerial photograph shows part of the downtown area which has been set up with tents and is wall-to-wall with people.

BET YOU DIDN'T KNOW...

Because of an error in surveying, Kentucky's southern border with Tennessee did not end up as a straight line as planned. This error happened in Simpson County on Nov. 14, 1780 when the survey party wandered off course from a marked beech tree. When the error was discovered, the surveyors reset their compasses rather than going back to correct the mistake. This point is known as "Black Jack Corner."

Kentucky has 120 counties. but 122 county seats and 122 courthouses. Kenton County has two county seats, Independence and Covington. The reason for this is that when Kenton County was formed from Campbell County in 1840, the act of establishment required that the county seat be located near the geographical center of the new county. However, even before the courthouse in Independence was completed in 1843, the residents of the more heavily populated northern area of the county found it to be too inconvenient to travel to Independence to conduct business and began using the old Covington City Hall as their courthouse. All of the county's main offices are located in the courthouse at Covington and only branch offices are located in the Independence courthouse.

Same situation in Campbell County with both Alexandria and Newport serving as county seats and each having its own courthouse. Alexandria was designated as the county seat in 1840 when Kenton County was formed from it but since Newport had been the county seat since 1794, the Newport residents became frustrated and built their own courthouse in 1844. The county's fiscal court and judicial offices are in the Newport courthouse, with other administrative offices located in Alexandria.

BET YOU DIDN'T KNOW...

The major crop of Calloway County is popcorn and 12 million pounds of it is produced annually. That is almost 10 percent of the US popcorn production.

Reelfoot Lake in Hickman County was formed by the earthquakes of 1811-12 along the New Madrid fault. This was the largest earthquake ever recorded and was felt as far way as Boston, MA. The quake was so powerful it changed the course of the Mississippi River and actually caused the river to flow backwards for a period of time. Most of Reelfoot Lake is in Tennessee.

Bet you didn't know...

The westernmost town in Kentucky is Hickman in Fulton County.

Kentucky was originally part of Fincastle County, VA and then became Kentucky County, VA in November 1780.

Graves County is the only county in Kentucky with four straight sides as boundaries.

From 1819-21 Hesler was the original seat of Owen County before it was moved to Owenton.

WATCH OUT!

This optical illusion makes it look as though this plane is getting ready to crash into the top of this building. The plane is actually about a quarter of a mile away getting ready to land at Louisville's Standiford Field. Thought it was a fun picture.

BET YOU DIDN'T KNOW...

Elk antlers can grow as much as one inch per day in summer

An average deer buck weighs around 150 pounds but a bull elk weighs around 700 pounds.

Midway College in Midway, Woodford County, is Kentucky's only women's college.

TRAIL OF TEARS

These Aztec dancers from Mexico City were very cooperative when asked to pose. They had just finished performing a series of dances during the annual Trail of Tears in Hopkinsville.

BET YOU DIDN'T KNOW...

There are no large, natural lakes in Kentucky. All are man-made. Kentucky Lake is the largest artificial lake in the eastern US.

The Shawnee Indians gave the name "Sheltowee" to Daniel Boone. It means "Big Turtle."

Bet you didn't know...

The Tennessee River is 650 miles long.

In 1774, Harrodsburg was known as Old Town.

The oldest man in the world, Elijah Blodsoe, died near Harrodsburg Nov. 11, 1902. He was 133 years old, had been married 13 times and fathered 74 children. This was reported in the *Clay City Times* on Nov. 13, 1902.

Bet you didn't know...

There are 176 school districts in Kentucky.

Flemingsburg is known as the "official covered bridge capitol of Kentucky."

COLVILLE COVERED BRIDGE

This covered bridge was located just outside of Paris in Bourbon County until it was washed away by floods. Although ruined by graffiti, the author wanted to get a picture of all 13 remaining covered bridges in Kentucky.

OFFUTT-COLE TAVERN

Name doesn't ring a bell? It didn't with the author either, but he just happened to run across this while driving on a back road in Woodford County.

This tavern was later known as the "Black Horse Tavern" and was operated as a tollgate house from 1848-1880. Richard Cole, the original owner, was the father of James, who was the father of Zerelda (Cole) James, who happened to be the mother of none other than the infamous Jesse and Frank James, robbers of trains and banks.

BET YOU DIDN'T KNOW...

Lincoln County was not named for Abraham Lincoln. Lincoln County was one of the original three counties formed from Kentucky County, VA in November 1780. Abraham Lincoln was not born until Feb. 12, 1809. A Revolutionary War hero, Gen. Benjamin Lincoln from Virginia is where the name comes from.

BET YOU DIDN'T KNOW...

Nelson County is spread over 437 square miles.

The last county to be formed in Kentucky was McCreary County in 1912.

Casey County was named for Col. William Casey, who was the great-grandfather of Samuel L. Clemens, better known as Mark Twain.

Bet you didn't know...

The First Kentucky Derby was won in 1875 by Aristides.

The last legal public hanging occurred Aug. 14, 1936 in a field in Owensboro, in Daviess County. A crowd of 10,000 showed up to see Rainey Bethea executed for rape. Because of this, a modification to the law took place in 1938 which required all executions to take place "within the walls of the state penitentiary."

TWO RIVERS BRIDGE

Located in Louisa, seat of Lawrence County, this bridge is listed in the Guiness Book of World Records as connecting two states, two counties, two towns and two school districts while spanning two rivers, the Tug and the Levisa Fork of the Big Sandy. The town on the right of the river is Fort Gay, WV.

BET YOU DIDN'T KNOW...

Inez, seat of Martin County, used to be known as Eden. When it was discovered that there was another town of the same name, it was changed to Inez in honor of the postmaster's daughter.

Simpson County has only one town which is Franklin.

MOONBOW OF CUMBERLAND FALLS

You are not going to believe this, but this picture was taken at around 11:30 at night! That's no lie. What you are looking at is not a rainbow, but a "moonbow." The only other place in the western hemisphere that has a moonbow is Victoria Falls in Africa. This can only be seen on a clear night when there is a full moon and even then it is not always visible.

When you see the moonbow with the naked eye, it appears as a simple white arc at the base of the falls. If you plan on taking a picture of this, you must not use a flash. There is not enough light being reflected off of the moonbow and a flash will overwhelm what little light is coming into the camera. Pocket cameras do not have this feature. This particular picture was taken by holding the shutter open for 4-1/2 minutes, most pocket cameras have a set shutter speed of 1/125 of a second.

BET YOU DIDN'T KNOW...

McLean County is the home of the first US soldier killed in WWI. His name was James B. Gresham, who died in the Battle of Sommerville Nov. 3, 1917.

US politician and statesman, Henry Clay was in Clark County when he made his first and last speeches.

Hancock County is where Abraham Lincoln had his first trial. He defended himself against charges that he was operating a ferry across the Ohio River with out a license. He had taken some men out in a rowboat to catch the ferry they had missed. Lincoln argued that he was not operating as a ferry since he did not go all the way across the river. He won the case.

WHITEHALL

This is the home of Cassius M. Clay, American abolitionist and statesman (not the boxer now known as Muhammad Ali), who was born in Madison County. Cassius Clay was an anti-slavery supporter and spent three terms in the Kentucky legislature from 1835-40. In 1845 he founded an anti-slavery publication called the True American which was published in Cincinnati, OH. His printing equipment was eventually destroyed by a pro-slavery mob and he later moved the publication to Louisville and changed the name of it to the Examiner.

In 1846 he was among the first to volunteer to fight in the Mexican War because he strongly opposed the invasion of Texas. During this time, he was taken prisoner for a period of time.

Cassius Clay served as US minister to Russia between 1861-69.

BET YOU DIDN'T KNOW...

Kentucky has over 765 miles of surveyed underground passages that are over one mile in length.

Bet you didn't know...

There are no operating smokestacks in Lexington or Fayette County. There is an ordinance prohibiting any type of smokestack. We can all breathe a little better about that.

Lincoln County has a few bragging rights. Among these are: the home of Kentucky's first governor; the first chartered school in the state; the first courthouse; the first bank west of the Alleghenies and the first circular race track in America.

TALLY HO!

These members of the Iroquois Hunt Club are off and running on their annual fox hunt.

BET YOU DIDN'T KNOW...

Rebecca Ruth Candies in Franklin County got its name from the founders, Rebecca Gooch and Ruth Hanly.

Alaska is the only state that has more navigable waterways than Kentucky.

Sky Bridge

Another popular attraction in the Red River Gorge is Sky Bridge. It is shown here surrounded by the beautiful fall colors.

Bet you didn't know...

Pine Mountain State Resort Park was Kentucky's first state park, being created in 1924.

Mt. Olivet, seat of Robertson County, may have been known as Hell's Half Acre.

The Civil War Monument on the courthouse lawn in Morgantown, seat of Butler County is the only one of its kind in Kentucky that honors both the North and the South.

CLAYS FERRY BRIDGES

The new Clays Ferry Bridge, which is part of I-75, dwarfs the other bridge crossing the Kentucky River at the Fayette-Madison County line. The new bridge is six lanes wide while the smaller bridge is only one lane. The smaller bridge is also about a quarter of a mile further back.

BET YOU DIDN'T KNOW...

The first "bank" in the Commonwealth was the Kentucky Insurance Co. which was started in 1802. It had the right to issue paper money which gave it "banking powers."

The Kentucky tourism industry is the second largest private employer in the state.

VALLEY PIKE COVERED BRIDGE

This is one of two covered bridges in Mason County, the other being the Dover Bridge which is shown elsewhere in the book. The Valley Pike Bridge is the only covered bridge in Kentucky that is privately owned.

BET YOU DIDN'T KNOW...

When the famous picture was taken of US Marines raising the American flag on Mt. Suribachi, Iwo Jima, Feb. 23, 1945, one of the Marines was a Kentuckian. He was Marine PFC Franklin R. Sousley, who was born and raised in the community of Hilltop in Fleming County. In the picture, he was the second from the left (holding the rifle). He was killed in action one month later.

In Kentucky, the Daniel Boone National Forest covers 687,000 acres in 21 counties. There are 500 miles of trails and 800 miles of roads.

ONE-ROOM SCHOOLHOUSE

This is all that remains of a one-room schoolhouse in West Liberty in Morgan County.

BET YOU DIDN'T KNOW...

Trimble County is 90 percent farmland.

Midway College was the first female orphan's school in the US.

During the Civil War, 22 Kentucky courthouses were burned.

Danville became Kentucky's first state capital in 1792.

In 1837, Clinton County needed to vote on a county seat so an election was held and the winner was ... Benjamin Dowell's Tavern! The town of Albany now covers that site.

Bet you didn't know...

In the 1860 US presidential election, the republican candidate, Abraham Lincoln, received only one vote in Trimble County.

The average annual rainfall in Kentucky varies from 52 inches in the south along the Tennessee border to only 41 inches in the north along the Ohio River.

Carl Brashear, from Sonora in Hardin County became the first African-American deep sea diver in US Naval history. He was not only the first African-American but was also the first amputee to earn the Navy's Master Diver certification.

Kentucky's Red River is 96 miles long.

The names of several Kentucky mining towns are actually abbreviations of the coal companies that operated there. Some examples are: "Seco" Southeast Coal, "Vicco" Virginia Iron, Coal & Coke and "Kayjay" Kentucky-Jellico Coal Co.

Some Kentucky communities have numbers for their names: "Eighty-eight," Barren County; "Nineteen," Ohio County; "Seventy-Six," Clinton County and "Number One," Wayne County. Some have "car" names: "Ford," Clark County and "Chevrolet," Harlan County. Some other interesting names of communities are: "Barnyard," Knox County; "Bug," Clinton County; "Goodluck," Metcalfe County; "Head of Grass," Lewis County and "Mousie," Knott County.

INTERESTING

Although it may look like the "Plains of Nazca" of South America or the "crop circles" of Europe, this aerial photo was taken somewhere between Mount Sterling and Morehead. The author just happened to be flying over and saw this one day after a fresh snow had fallen the day before. He thought it was kind of interesting because it can really only be seen from the air.

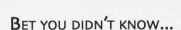

BET YOU DIDN'T KNOW...

Sixty Kentuckians have been awarded the Congressional Medal of Honor.

The Cumberland River is the only river in Kentucky that flows south, then changes course and flows north.

Bet you didn't know...

The world's largest small mouth bass was caught at Kentucky's Dale Hollow Lake. The bass weighted in at 11 pounds, 15 ounces.

The western tip of Kentucky is known as the Jackson Purchase. It is comprised of eight counties and covers 8,500 square miles. The land was purchased in 1818 for $300,000. That's just little over $35 for a square mile of land!

Kentucky barbecue takes its name from the Spanish conquistador word "barbacoa," which is what they called the green wood frame on which the Carib Indians roasted meat over an open fire.

Welcome to the *Horse Capital* of the *World*

BET YOU DIDN'T KNOW...

The Green River drains more water into the Ohio River than any other stream in Kentucky.

Only three Kentucky counties have county seats whose names match that of the county itself: Greenup, Harlan and Henderson.

KENTUCKY-AMERICAN WATER CO.

This water tank, constructed in 1987, sits at the intersection of I-64/I-75 in Lexington. The mural was painted by Eric Henn of Ohio. The tank is 36 feet high, has a diameter of 120 feet, and holds 3,000,000 gallons of water. The mural covers 18,000 square feet and Eric went through 250 brushes and 267 gallons of paint. The mural cost $35,000 and was covered entirely by donations.

PENN'S STORE

This is the oldest country store in America continually owned and operated by the same family. The building was constructed in 1845 and has been in the Penn family since 1850. On November 7, 1882, this also became the first post office for Rollings, Kentucky.

This store is unique in another way as well. The property sits in three counties. One county line runs right down the middle of the store. There is a wood/coal stove in the middle of the room. If you walk around the right hand side of it you are in Boyle County, but if you walk around the left hand side of it you are in Casey County. If you walk up the hill behind the store, you will be in Marion County.

This store has been featured in Newspapers and magazines and was even the backdrop for a *Playboy Magazine* shooting session.

BET YOU DIDN'T KNOW...

In 1961 the first Kentucky Invitational Wrestling Tournament was won by the Kentucky School for the Blind.

There are 16 State Police posts in Kentucky.

KNOTT HOLE, KENTUCKY

And you thought you had been everywhere and seen it all!

BET YOU DIDN'T KNOW...

Knott County is the only county in Kentucky that does not have a river either within its boundaries or bordering it.

Knox County was the home of two Kentucky governors. They were James Black, who governed in 1919 and Flem Sampson, serving as governor from 1927-31.

Less than 2 percent of the land in Leslie County can be used for farming due to its mountainous terrain.

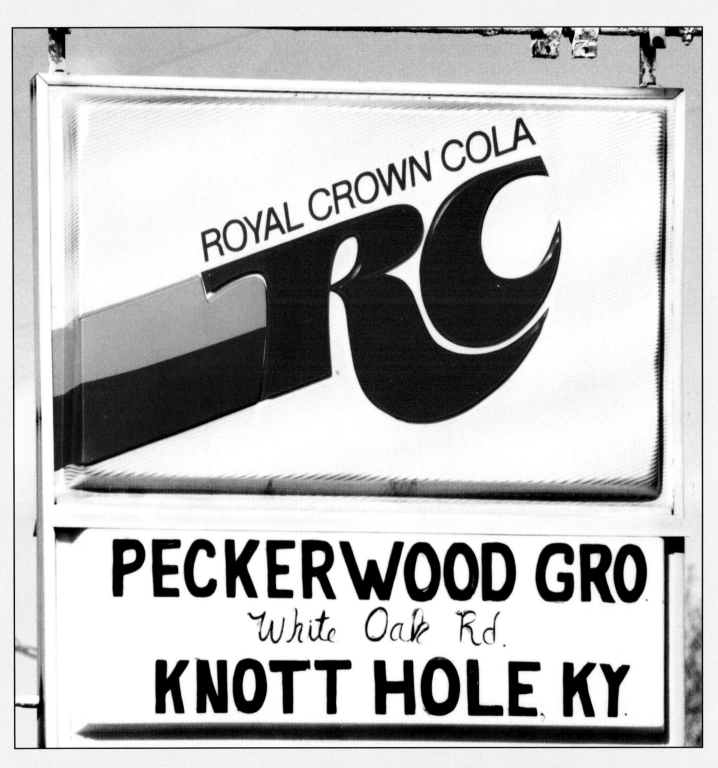

OH, THE SUN SHINES BRIGHT ...

Some of the cast members of The Stephen Foster Story are wearing their antebellum dresses during the outdoor performance in Bardstown.

BET YOU DIDN'T KNOW...

The first licensed commercial radio station in Kentucky was Louisville's WHAS.

Three of Kentucky's major rivers have their headwaters in Letcher County. They are the Levisa Fork of the Big Sandy, the Cumberland and the North Fork of the Kentucky.

Perry County had the last one-room school in Kentucky. It closed in 1989.

Bet you didn't know...

Former University of Kentucky men's basketball coach Adolph Rupp played college basketball for the University of Kansas Jayhawks from 1921-23. During those three seasons, Rupp did not score a single point.

In 1917, the town of Lynch, in Harlan, County was home to the world's largest coal camp and coal tipple. On Feb. 12, 1923, the miners in this camp set a world record for coal production during a nine-hour shift by mining 12,820 tons of coal.

"Crooked Nose" Jack McCall was hanged in South Dakota for the 1876 murder of Wild Bill Hickock. At that time, McCall's mother, Mary McCall was a housekeeper at the Merchants Hotel in Louisville.

BLUE MOON OF KENTUCKY

Blue Moon of Kentucky was a bluegrass song written and played by the late Bill Monroe and the Bluegrass Boys. Do you know what a "blue moon" is? Have you ever heard the expression, "Once in a blue moon?"

BET YOU DIDN'T KNOW...

A full moon usually occurs only once a month. However, every couple of years a full moon occurs twice in the same month. When this occurs, the second full moon of the month is known as the "blue moon." This expression "once in a blue moon" means that something does not happen very often.

Harlan County has parts of four mountain ranges within its borders. There are Pine, Black, Little Black and Stone Mountains.

STAINED GLASS WINDOWS

Y ou don't see many churches with stained glass windows anymore. This is the inside of the First Christian Church in Winchester.

BET YOU DIDN'T KNOW...

The year that the most new counties in Kentucky were formed was 1799, 12 new counties were formed that year.

The first American oil well is at Burkesville in Cumberland County.

Harrison county is 92 percent agricultural.

In 1834, Hazard, county seat of Perry County was named Perry but the residents preferred to call it Hazard, so in 1854 the name was changed to Hazard.

The first men's basketball coach for the University of Kentucky was Leander E. Andrus, who coached the team in 1904. So far, 19 others have coached the Wildcat basketball team.

The original county seat of Bath County was Catlett's Flat, but was moved to Owingsville in 1811.

The Bank of Columbia, in Adair County was robbed by five members of the notorious Jesse James Gang on April 29, 1872. The cashier was killed.

MT. STERLING AIRPORT

BET YOU DIDN'T KNOW...

The town of Corbin, originally named Lynn Camp, is right at the juncture of three counties. So close, in fact that the town itself is in Whitley County, but some of its suburbs are in Knox County while other suburbs are in Laurel County.

There were 41 code duello duels fought in Kentucky between 1790 and 1867. Sixteen men died as a result and no one was prosecuted for murder. Code duello duels had very stringent rules and usually no one ever got hurt. Duels without rules were known as de facto duels and were usually nothing more than what amounted to a street fight. No records were kept of these, but would bet that there were more than 41.

159

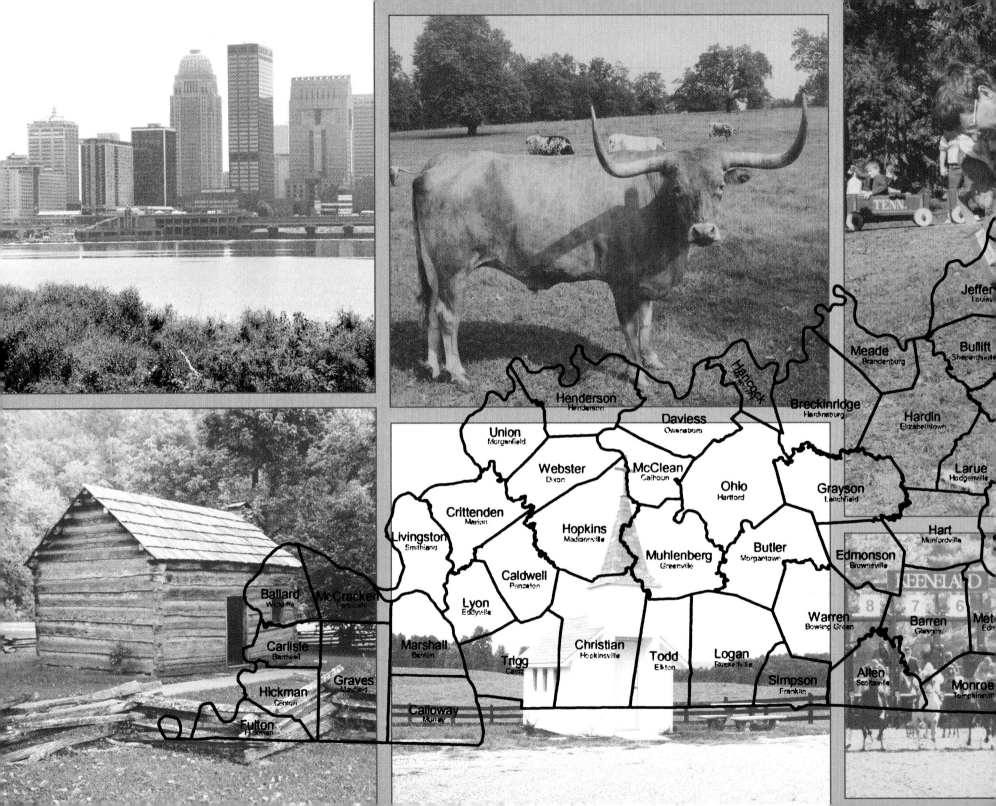

Jefferson
Louisville

Meade
Brandenburg

Bullitt
Shepherdsville

Henderson
Henderson

Hancock

Breckinridge
Hardinsburg

Hardin
Elizabethtown

Union
Morganfield

Daviess
Owensboro

Larue
Hodgenville

Webster
Dixon

McClean
Calhoun

Ohio
Hartford

Grayson
Leitchfield

Crittenden
Marion

Hopkins
Madisonville

Butler
Morgantown

Edmonson
Brownsville

Hart
Munfordville

Livingston
Smithland

Muhlenberg
Greenville

KEENELAND

Ballard
Wickliffe

McCracken
Paducah

Caldwell
Princeton

8 7 6

Carlisle
Bardwell

Lyon
Eddyville

Warren
Bowling Green

Barren
Glasgow

Met
Edm

Marshall
Benton

Christian
Hopkinsville

Todd
Elkton

Logan
Russellville

Allen
Scottsville

Hickman
Clinton

Graves
Mayfield

Trigg
Cadiz

Simpson
Franklin

Monroe
Tompkinsville

Fulton
Hickman

Calloway
Murray

ABOVE PARIS

by ROBERT CAMERON

A new collection of aerial
photographs of Paris, France

with text by
PIERRE SALINGER

ANDRE DEUTSCH
London WC 1, England

MAINTENON

(Opposite) VAUX-LE-VICOMTE

TABLE OF CONTENTS

Such a book as this does not reach publication without more than the usual amount of
cooperation from many people. So, for their encouragement and expertise we thank the following:

Francois Benoist, Guy Buffet, Robert Burger, Todd Cameron, Ken Cellini, Jean-Louis Clément, Phillippe-Marie Denis,
Michel Drucker, Yves Groetschel, Alice Harth, Suzanne Lawlor, Mary Martinet, Patricia O'Grady,
Dolly Patterson, Julian Peabody, Gilbert Rosati, Eric Steinle, and Henry Struck.

Helicopter Pilot Patrick Le Boedec of Professional Air System, Jean Créon Mgr.

And for very special expertise and talent
both on the ground and in the air, Josabeth Drucker.

ANDRE
DEUTSCH

First published in Great Britain in 1985 by
André Deutsch Limited, 105 Great Russell Street, London WC 1

Copyright ©1984 by Robert W. Cameron and Company

ISBN 0-233-97794-5

Book design by
JANE OLAUG KRISTIANSEN

Typography by Reeder Type Inc.   Color film processing by Colortec, Paris   Color Separation and Printing by Dai Nippon Printing Co., Tokyo, Japan
Cameras: Pentax 6x7 System

I first came to Paris in December of 1925. My mother decided it was a good occasion to have me baptized as a Catholic. She chose, not just any church, but Notre-Dame Cathedral. I was six months old at the time, but my feelings about Paris today lead me to believe that there must be some kind of osmosis at work in the being of a young child. Otherwise, why would Paris continue to haunt me long after as a place I wanted to see, and where eventually I wanted to live?

I returned to Paris almost 36 years later, to help advance President Kennedy's visit to France soon after his election. I will never forget the impact the city made on me the day I landed in April of 1961. I had the feeling I had arrived, not just in a city, but in a living museum, reflecting 23 centuries of history.

Finally, in 1968, after Robert Kennedy was killed, this second tragedy of the Kennedys in my life in 5 years, I felt the need to get away from America for a while. The logical choice was Paris. I have been here ever since.

In November of 1983 I made a brief trip to San Francisco to give some lectures at my alma mater, the University of San Francisco, and it was at that time that I met Bob Cameron. He had just finished *Above Yosemite*, a stunning work on one of the most beautiful regions of the United States. It was the culmination of a series of "Above" books—San Francisco, Los Angeles, Hawaii, Washington, D.C., and London. He told me he wanted to do *Above Paris*, and asked if I would work with him. I immediately said yes. Yet there were unexpected problems. Over the past two decades security has been considerably tightened in Paris. Authorization to fly above the city in a helicopter is one of the things it is almost impossible to obtain. But I tried. In January of 1984 I had my first appointment with the Préfet de Police, Guy Fougier, to apply for the necessary permissions. I took with me a copy of

Above London, as my best argument. M. Fougier was enthusiastic about the idea, but even with the power he had to grant authorization, he admitted it would be very difficult.

By April, however, the Prefecture was so encouraging that I advised Bob to come to Paris. Throughout the month, Paris had some of the most beautiful weather it has ever seen in April. Finally, at the end of the month, our authorization came—but for just a single hour of flight at from 1,200 to 2,000 feet, depending on the location. If that were not discouraging enough, now another factor intervened: the weather turned sour. Bob took what photographs he could, and returned home. It seemed that *Above Paris* was doomed.

I soon discovered, however, that Bob had not wasted his time. During his stay he had taken a helicopter to the château-rich section outside of Paris. And in the brief half-hour over Paris he had gotten some stunning shots of the capitol. We decided to make a mock-up of the book with what he had. There was still a way to get authorization for the critical photographs we needed.

The mock-up arrived in Paris on June 4, and the following day I had an invitation to lunch with some high government officials. We were only eight around the table, so that after lunch I had a few moments to show them the proposed book and to explain our problem. They were taken with the project and agreed to instruct the proper authorities with the permissions. The authorizations were received within 48 hours. This time Bob would be allowed to fly at a lower altitude to give his eye and his camera a clearer view of Paris.

The result is glowing, for Paris in its entirety has never been seen quite like this. The Ile de la Cité with its imposing Cathedral, the familiar but ever new Eiffel Tower, the modern Pompidou Center in its bright blue and red standing in the

middle of an historic and traditional neighborhood, the Arc de Triomphe and the Champs-Elysées—all are seen here in an entirely new dimension, and they add a new perspective to France's capitol. This unique photographic collection reflects the long history of France, going back three centuries before Christ, through years of war and revolution, to the time when it became the cultural center of the world, an intellectual beacon to artists, musicians, architects, scientists from around the globe. One can understand why virtually every modern American composer came to Paris to do their early work, why writers like Ernest Hemingway, Scott Fitzgerald and Henry Miller made Paris their home. That ancient Paris has little changed, although it has acquired a bit of modern look with the skyscraper complex at La Défense, the high rise office buildings, apartments and hotels on the banks of the Seine, and the towering Tour Montparnasse, the tallest bulding in Paris, opened in 1973.

From the window of my apartment on the Rue de Rivoli the view is like a living history book. Looking from left to right, I can see Notre-Dame Cathedral, the Louvre, the Jeu de Paume, the church of Sainte-Clotilde, the National Assembly, the Dome of the Invalides, the Tuileries Gardens, the Grand Palais, and the Eiffel Tower. In seeing this panorama of Gothic, Renaissance, and modern structures, one relives the times of kings and empire, the Revolution of 1789, the uprising of the Paris Commune of 1871, the two world wars and the spectacular liberation of Paris of August 25, 1944, the student uprisings of May of 1968. But one also sees the neighborhoods that became the paintings of Toulouse-Lautrec, of Monet and Manet, and the inspiration of artists like Picasso and Chagall. Paris is the city of wonder. This book consecrates that wonder.

PIERRE SALINGER
Paris, July 8, 1984

LE PLAN DE LA VILLE, CITE, VNIVERSITE ET FAVXBOVRGS DE PARIS AVEC LA DESCRIPTION DE SON ANTIQVI ET SINGVLARITES

LA RIVIERE DE SEINE

BIRD'S-EYE PERSPECTIVE, HISTORICAL AND MODERN

CITY PLAN OF PARIS DRAWN IN 1615

On the left is a city plan of Paris drawn in 1615. In the middle of the Seine, one can see the Ile de la Cité, with the Notre-Dame Cathedral, the Palais de la Justice, and the Conciergerie. Behind the Ile de la Cité are two small uninhabited islands which have been joined and are now the fashionable Ile Saint-Louis. In the background, on the left, is the prison of La Bastille, assaulted by mobs on July 14, 1789, at the beginning of the French Revolution. On the right is a view of the islands of the Seine.

On this page is a reproduction of the first aerial photograph ever taken. It was made by the famous Nadar, in 1854, who worked from a balloon. He is shown here in its basket. On the opposite page, is the same area, after 130 years of expansion.

PARYS

In the beginning of the seventeenth century, after a series of epidemics of the plague, a decision was made to build a new hospital. It was constructed outside the walls of Paris to protect the citizens from contagion. This mid-seventeenth century drawing shows the Hospital St-Louis along with its beautiful chapel. On the right, now well within the city, is the same hospital, which continues to be an important medical center.

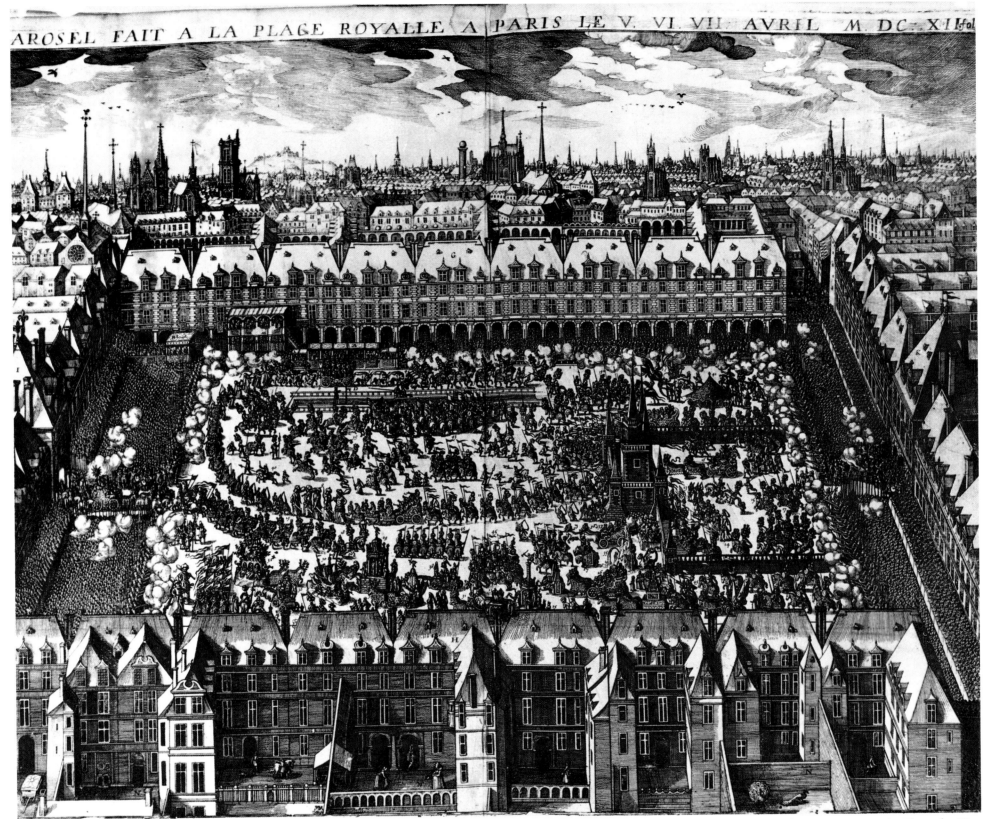

AROSEL FAIT A LA PLAGE ROYALLE A PARIS LE V. VI. VII. AVRIL M. DC. XII.

Above, is a drawing by Mathieu Merian showing the inauguration of the Place Royale in April of 1612. The Place is filled with musicians, cavaliers, and an enormous crowd which came to celebrate a double marriage—that of King Louis XIII and that of his sister. The Place Royale was situated in the heart of the Marais, then Paris' most fashionable neighborhood where aristocrats, royalty, and the rich financiers built opulent homes. There was a period when the Marais was abandoned to small artisans, but, recently, many of the old homes have been restored.

In 1800, the Place Royale was renamed the Place des Vosges. In the photo on the right, one can see how little the old Place Royale has changed, how the old buildings, which surround the square, still reflect their historic past. On the lower left side of the photo, we see one of the fashionable homes of the seventeenth century, the Hôtel de Bethune Sully, purchased in 1634 by Maximilien de Bethune, Duke of Sully, a former minister of Henri IV.

PORTRAIT DV MAGNIFIQVE BASTIMENT DE LA MAISON DE VILLE DE PARIS.

Mathieu Merian's engraving of the Hôtel de Ville (City Hall) of Paris was made in 1645 during the Feast of Saint Jean. Jacques Hilairet wrote, "The Hôtel de Ville of Paris has been the palace of all the revolutions; the rallying place for all national emotions. To tell its history is to tell the history of the nation."

The first municipality of Paris was created in 1246 and in 1357 it was moved into a building on this same site. The version in the drawing was built during the reign of Francois I by an Italian architect known as le Boccador. In May 1871, the Hôtel de Ville in the engraving was destroyed during the Commune.

The new Hôtel de Ville, constructed between 1873 and 1883, seen in the photograph on the right, is a copy of the previous version. The mayor of Paris, Jacques Chirac, whose offices are here, was elected by universal suffrage in 1977. On the upper right of the photograph, one can see the tip of the Ile de la Cité, and in the upper middle of the picture is the beginning of the Ile Saint-Louis.

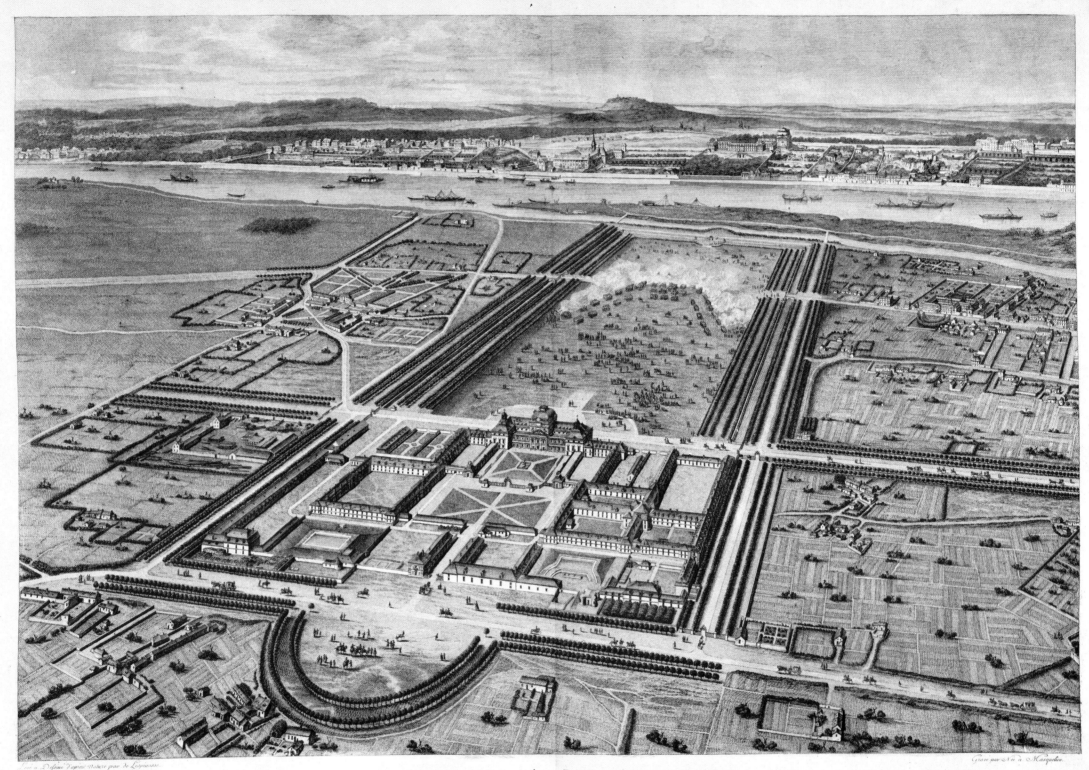

PLAN PERSPECTIF DE L'ECOLE ROYALE MILITAIRE

Isle de France n° 57.

In 1778, the French artist, Lespinasse, did this drawing of the Ecole Royale Militaire. On the right, one can see how things have changed. The same area, seen from the air, shows one stupendous difference; that is, the presence of the Eiffel Tower, which was inaugurated in 1889 during the Universal Exposition of that year. The Ecole Royale Militaire, which was constructed in the mid-eighteenth century still stands as one of France's most beautiful architectural creations. Between it and the Eiffel Tower are the lovely trees and gardens of the Champ-de-Mars, the site of huge demonstrations during the Revolution and site of the first launching of a hydrogen balloon in 1783.

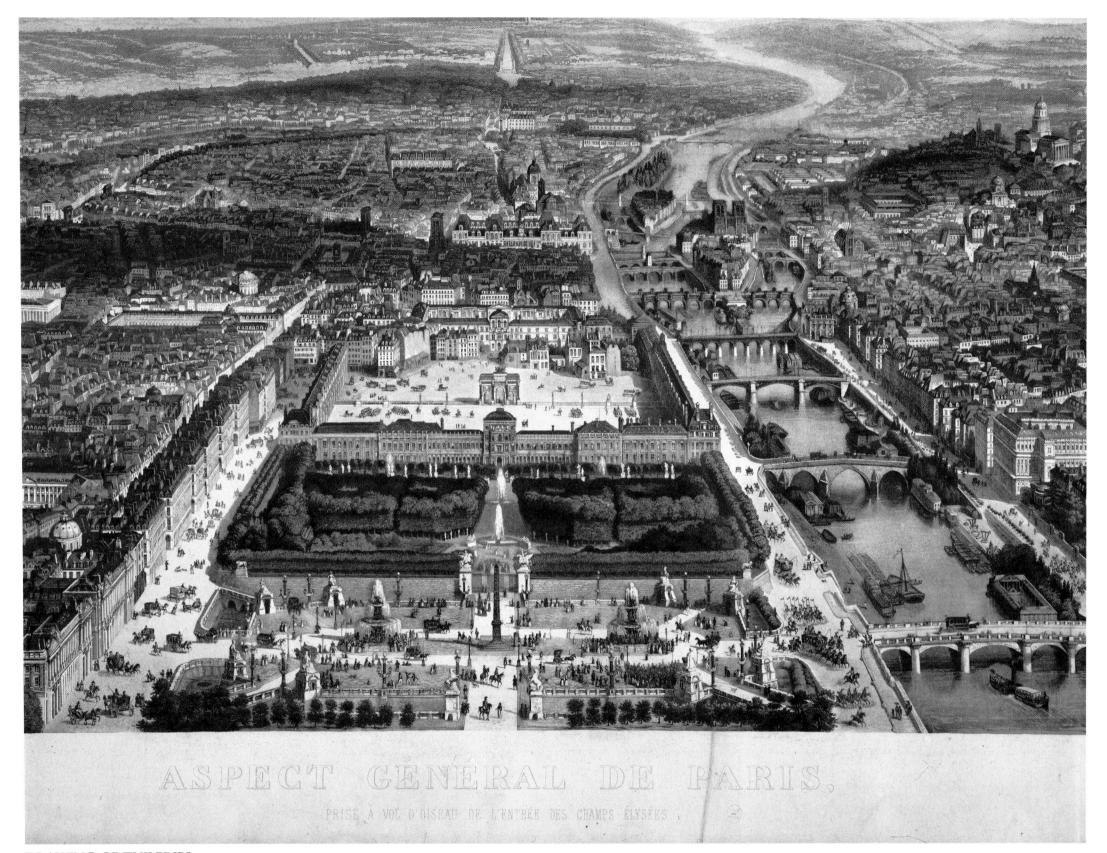

ASPECT GÉNÉRAL DE PARIS,

PRISE À VOL D'OISEAU DE L'ENTRÉE DES CHAMPS-ÉLYSÉES,

DRAWING OF TUILERIES

Above, is an early nineteenth century drawing of the Tuileries Gardens dominated by the Palais des Tuileries, which was built in the sixteenth century by Catherine di Medici. The royal castle was destroyed during the uprising of the Paris Commune in 1871. All that remains today are the two pavilions on the left and on right sides of the château, the Pavillon de Flore, and the Pavillon de Marsan. Behind the royal castle one can see the Louvre and the Place du Carousel, which, at one time, was filled with private homes.

(Opposite) This is an unusual picture of the Place de la Concorde in that scaffolding is rising from the center to provide reviewing stands for the Bastille Day celebration on July 14. On the right is a view of the Tuileries Gardens.

PLACE DE LA BASTILLE

It was here in the Place de la Bastille that the French Revolution was born. The Bastille, a prison finished in 1382, was assaulted by a mob on July 14, 1789. It was soon captured, its prisoners were freed, and the building was destroyed. But, the Place de la Bastille has remained the gathering point for protest and celebration by popular factions in France.

In the middle of the Place, a 171-foot column was erected in memory of the Parisians killed in July of 1830. There was a huge mob here on May 10, 1981, when President François Mitterrand was elected. With him, he brought the French left to power.

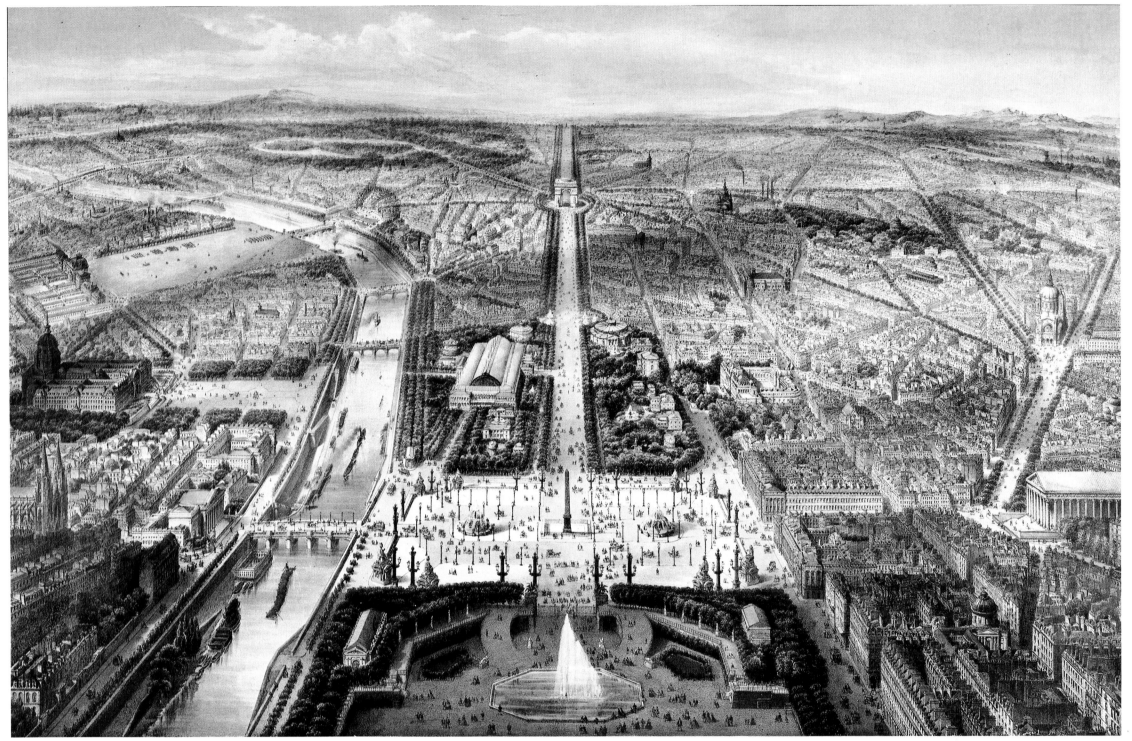

CONCORDE, CHAMPS-ELYSEES
Above, an 1865 drawing of the Champs Elysées. In the foreground, the end of the Tuileries Gardens and the Place de la Concorde. At right, the same view but shot from a little farther away.

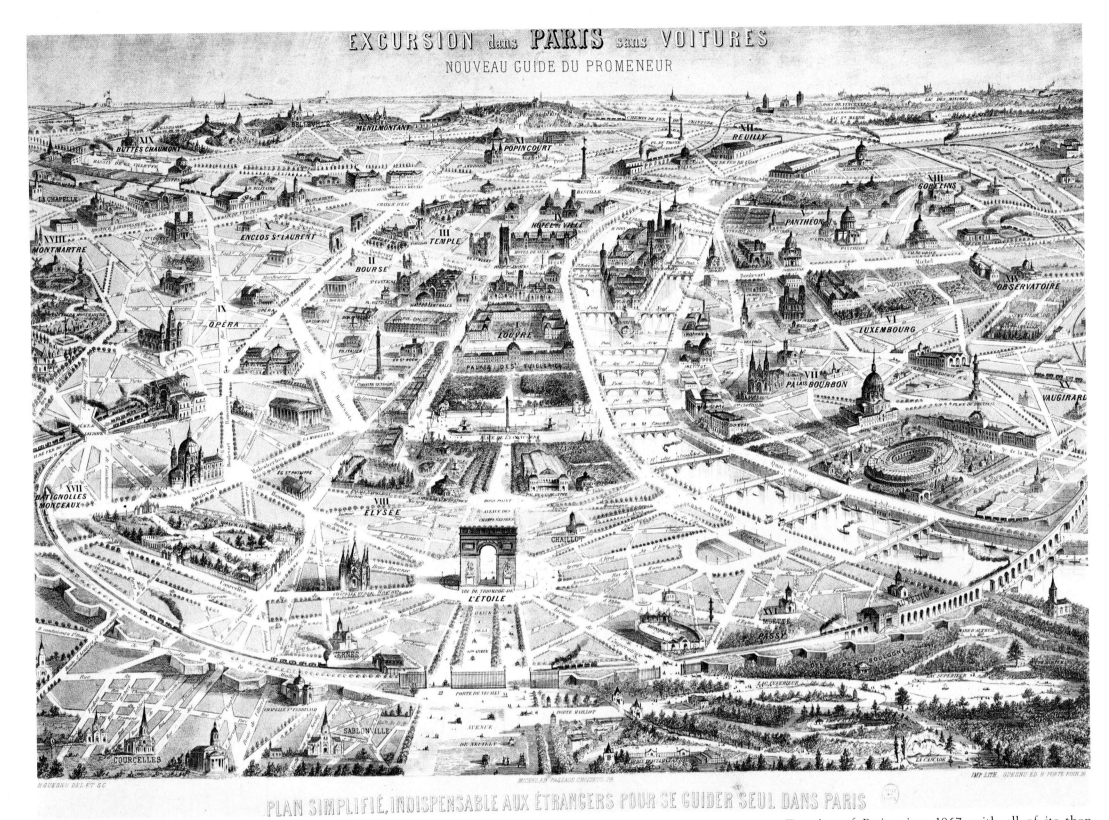

Drawing of Paris, circa 1867, with all of its then famous landmarks identified.

LE PREMIER KILOMÈTRE BOUCLÉ EN AEROPLANE

Le prix Deutsch-Archdeacon de 50.000 francs gagné par M. Henri Farman sur le champ de manœuvres d'Issy-les-Moulineaux : instantané pris au moment du retour de l'aviateur entre les poteaux d'arrivée.

Above, is a photo of the British pilot, Henri Farman, son of the Paris correspondent of the London newspaper, *The Standard*. Farman made one of the first flights, in 1908, at Issy-les-Moulineaux. The flight (the first specific "point-to-point") lasted one minute and twenty-eight seconds and covered a little over 1,000 yards at about 30 miles per hour.

On the right is the Paris heliport which is in Issy-les-Moulineaux, on the west end of Paris. It is from here that we flew to photograph *Above Paris.*

POMPIDOU CENTER

The Georges Pompidou Center, a modern and extremely colorful addition to one of Paris' more traditional neighborhoods, has attracted massive crowds. Heavily criticized at first, as was the Eiffel Tower when it was built, the Pompidou Center has now taken its place as one of the French capital's most popular attractions. At the front of the Center is a large piazza constantly filled with mimes, fire-eaters, jugglers, and street musicians. The Center includes the National Museum of Modern Art, the Public Information Library, the Industrial Design Center, and the Institute of Acoustic and Musical Research (IRCAM), where new technology and music are combined. The Center was opened in 1977, three years after President Georges Pompidou, who created the idea, died. Above, is a photo taken in 1951, which shows the demolition that was necessary to make room for the Pompidou Center.

OLD LES HALLES, RUNGIS

Paris' giant wholesale produce market, called Les Halles (above), was located in the heart of the city until 1969. It was made up of ten huge halls designed by the architect Baltard and constructed between 1854 and 1866, with two more halls added in 1936. At the far side of the halls in the photo is the rotunda of the Paris commercial trade center.

The vast market with all its activity finally outgrew its inner-city setting and was moved to more spacious quarters at Rungis (opposite, top) near Orly airport. The lower color photograph shows the area of Paris vacated by Les Halles: behind the trade center, a hotel, residential and sports complex under construction, and the Forum, already completed, with its boutiques and museum. To the left of the construction site, one of Paris' loveliest churches, Saint-Eustache.

33

INSIDE THE PERIPHERIQUE

ILE SAINT-LOUIS AND ILE DE LA CITE

This is an overall view of two historic islands in the Seine, the Ile Saint-Louis, in the foreground, and, in the background, the Ile de la Cité, the historic cradle of Paris. It was here, in the third century B.C., that the Parisii tribe settled, thus beginning the Gallo-Roman Period and the founding of the city of Paris. Today, the Ile de la Cité contains Notre-Dame Cathedral and the complex of the Palais de Justice.

Both Islands are linked to the left and to the right banks of the Seine by a series of bridges, some built as early as the seventeenth century. On the Ile Saint-Louis, there remain some sumptuous houses, for example, the Hôtel Lambert built in 1640.

35

PLACE DAUPHINE—ACADEMIE FRANCAISE

This little piece of land between the complex of the Palais de Justice and the tip of the Ile de la Cité is called the Place Dauphine. It was the idea of Henri IV, in the beginning of the seventeenth century, to build a triangular park in honor of the Dauphin (the heir apparent to the throne) who became Louis XIII.

In the background, on the right, are the French Institute and the headquarters of the French Academies which honor the best in writing, science, the arts, and political sciences. Before his death in 1661, Cardinal Mazarin bequeathed the money to build a college for sixty students. But, after the Revolution, Napoléon transformed the building into headquarters for the Institute. The most known of the Academies is the Académie Francaise, with only forty members, the majority of whom are writers. When one dies, the remaining members elect the successor. There has been only one woman admitted to the Academy, Marguerite Yourcenar. The Institute also includes Cardinal Mazarin's rich and extensive library.

PONT DES ARTS—PONT NEUF

(Opposite) In the foreground is the Pont des Arts, a pedestrian bridge which cuts across the Seine from the Louvre to the French Institute. Behind the Pont des Arts, cutting across the Seine and the Ile de la Cité, is the Pont Neuf, which, despite its name meaning "new bridge," is the oldest bridge in Paris, dating back to 1578. In the background, stands Notre-Dame Cathedral.

37

CONCORDE-MADELEINE

The Place de la Concorde, in the foreground, Paris' largest square, an area of twenty-one acres, is replete with history. Originally, it was named after Louis XV, and a statue was placed there to honor the King. The statue was torn down and destroyed in 1792, during the French Revolution, and the guillotine was installed there.

In 1836, in the middle of the Concorde, Louis-Philippe erected an ancient obelisk from Luxor, Egypt, given to France by Mehemet-Ali, the Viceroy of Egypt. The obelisk continues to occupy its original place. It was on the Place de la Concorde that Louis XVI, Marie-Antoinette, Robespierre, and more than a thousand other persons were decapitated.

RUE DE RIVOLI

In the foreground is the Rue de Rivoli, one of Napoléon's projects, which was finished in the middle of the nineteenth century. Seen below and above an arcade are a succession of buildings uniformly designed in the Empire style. Behind the Rue de Rivoli, one can see the Place Vendôme, with the Rue de la Paix and its fancy jewelry shops, such as Cartier, running north out of the Place. On the left, in the rear, is the Paris Opera.

RUE DE RIVOLI AND PLACE VENDOME

The Rue de Rivoli was built between 1800 and 1835. Its north side is the most cohesive example in Paris of the architecture inspired by the French Empire. Across the street from these majestic buildings, which are mostly apartments, are located the Louvre and the Tuileries Gardens. Behind the Rue de Rivoli is the famed Place Vendôme, which was first established at the end of the seventeenth century. There stood the statue of Louis XIV, which was destroyed during the Revolution and re-placed by the famed Vendôme column made up of 1,200 melted cannons seized in battle by Napoléon in 1805 from the Russians and the Austrians. The column was erected in honor of the soldiers who won the Battle of Austerlitz. It was torn down during the Paris Commune in 1871 but was put up again in 1873. This time, a statue of Napoléon I, dressed as a Roman Emperor, was placed on top of the column.

NOTRE-DAME

It has been said of Notre-Dame: "It is not the highest, largest, or richest church, but, there is none more perfect." Construction of the Cathedral started in 1163, and Pope Alexander III laid the first stone. The construction took only seventy-five years, which was exceptional for that time. Since then, Notre-Dame has been intimately linked with the history of France. Napoléon was proclaimed Emperor there in 1804. The Cathedral was badly damaged during the Revolution. It was not until 1845 that Viollet-le-Duc undertook seventeen years of restoration work. Behind Notre-Dame, one can see the Préfecture de Police, Paris' police headquarters, located like the Cathedral, on the Ile de la Cité.

THE GRAND PALAIS AND THE PETIT PALAIS

(Opposite) The Grand Palais and the Petit Palais were built for the Paris Universal Exposition of 1900. At the left side of the Grand Palais is the Palais de la Découverte, a center for scientific instruction. It includes scientific exhibits and a planetarium. The Grand Palais and the Petit Palais are today the sites for prestigious art and other types of exhibits.

ROND-POINT DES CHAMPS-ELYSEES

The Rond-Point des Champs-Elysées was designed in 1670 by the famed French architect of gardens, André Le Nôtre. At that time, the Rond-Point was one end of the Champs-Elysées, which only ran to the Place Royale, the Concorde of today. But, in the eighteenth century, the Champs-Elysées was lengthened to reach the Étoile, where the Arc de Triomphe now stands.

FRONT DE SEINE

Some of the modern apartment buildings, office blocks, and hotels, which have recently sprung up on the left bank of the Seine River, can be seen in this photograph. Behind them is the Eiffel Tower. Also evident, are the roofs of the Grand Palais, the Petit Palais, and the Church of the Madeleine.

EIFFEL TOWER

(Opposite) Built for the Universal Exposition of 1889, the Eiffel Tower is the creation of the engineer, Gustave Eiffel, who also built the metalwork for the interior of the Statue of Liberty. Artists and intellectuals of the time attacked the project as "useless and monstrous." But, today, it remains Paris' number one tourist attraction. The Eiffel Tower, which is more than 1000 feet high since television relays were added, is composed of 15,000 pieces of metal and 2,500,000 rivets. In 1982 and 1983, the Eiffel Tower was refurbished and now contains an elegant restaurant, the Jules Verne. To the left of the Eiffel Tower is the Champ-de-Mars. Behind it, across the Seine, is the Maison de la Radio, headquarters of Radio France.

THE INVALIDES

(Opposite) The Invalides, one of the most spectacular points of interest in Paris, was originally the work of Louis XIV, who had it built between 1671 and 1676 as a barracks for 4,000 wounded soldiers. It was here, on July 14, 1789, that the mob first attacked. They overpowered the guards and took almost 30,000 rifles for the assault on the Bastille, which launched the French Revolution. Here the body of Napoleon was returned in 1840. His remains were kept under the Cupola until a specially-designed tomb was ready in 1861.

The famed Esplanade, in front, was constructed between 1704 and 1720. It is almost 600 yards long and 300 yards wide. In the back of the Invalides are the Church of Saint-Louis-des-Invalides and the Dome Church, also constructed under the reign of Louis XIV. In 1937, 350,000 sheets of gold were used to gild the dome. The total weight of the gold was only fourteen pounds.

SEMINAIRE DES MISSIONS ETRANGERES

The Seminaire des Missions Etrangères was first built in the seventeenth century. It still exists in the same building with its vast and original gardens. This area is only one example of the hidden gardens which dot Paris. These are, for the most part, unknown to people in the street, because they cannot see past the walls or the building fronts which hide them.

MUSEE RODIN

The building, which houses the Rodin Museum, was constructed in 1728. Marshall de Biron purchased the structure, and it became the Hôtel Biron. After Marshall de Biron's death, just before the Revolution, the house served a series of functions: as a dance hall, as the headquarters of the Papal legation, and as the residence of the Ambassador of the Tsar.

In 1904, the buildings at the rear of the garden were converted to a grammar school. The house was made available to artists. The celebrated French sculptor, Auguste Rodin, lived there until his death in 1917, after which it was converted to a museum in his honor. The gardens were restored to their eighteenth century design. On the left of the photograph is the Invalides.

PLACE DE LA REPUBLIQUE

Situated in the working class district of Paris, the Place de la République has, at its center, a monument to the French Republic, created by the sculptor, Morice, and erected in 1883. On the right, the Verines Barracks was built in 1854 to house 2,000 men. Most of the important labor demonstrations take place in marches between the Bastille and the Place de la République.

MAISON DE LA RADIO

The Maison de la Radio, built in 1963, houses all of the different elements of Radio France, the state-owned radio network. The interior of the building, which includes concert halls, is a veritable maze, as difficult to navigate as the Pentagon.

The scaled-down replica of Bartholdi's masterpiece which graces the New York harbor, the Statue of Liberty, appears distinctly on the point of the island in the Seine at the lower right corner.

ST-GERVAIS

(Opposite) This is a rather wide-angle shot of the modern and colorful Pompidou Center which stands in the middle of the Beaubourg section of Paris. In the foreground is the Hôtel de Ville. In the back, in the center, is the Church of St-Gervais-St-Protais which has stood on this site since the sixteenth century. This form of architecture extended from the fifteenth to the seventeenth centuries. The classical facade of this church was the first one built in Paris.

THE CLUNY MUSEUM

(Opposite) What is now the Cluny Museum was built on a site which was occupied, in the third century, by a Gallo-Roman public bath. The site was purchased in the early fourteenth century by the Abbot of Cluny, who built a residence there and transformed it, in 1500, to its present design. The Museum was founded after the French Revolution and is devoted to art of the Middle Ages. It is fascinating to see some of the remains of the public baths.

THE MOSQUE

The Mosque of Paris, dominated by a minaret, was built just after World War I. Paris' Moslem population has grown considerably in the last fifty years, particularly through the influx of immigrant workers from North Africa. In the background, are the Botanical Gardens.

THE MONTSOURIS PARK

The Montsouris Park, planned and completed between 1868 and 1878, has a replica of the home of the Bey of Tunis, which was offered to the city for the 1867 Exposition. The Park has continuously attracted many painters. The famed Georges Braque lived in an apartment bordering the park.

THE PANTHEON

(Opposite) The Panthéon, built at the direction of Louis XV, was started in 1758 as the church for the Sainte-Geneviève cloister. Sainte-Geneviève is the religious patron of Paris. The church was not finished until 1789. In 1791, the revolutionary leaders decided that the Panthéon should house the ashes of the great figures of French history. Voltaire, Jean-Jacques Rousseau, and Victor Hugo are there. Included also is Jean Moulin, a hero of the French resistance, killed by the Germans during World War II. In the foreground is one of Paris' highest-rated secondary schools, the Lycée Henri IV, located in what remains of the cloister.

UNESCO

The modern building in the foreground is the headquarters of UNESCO, the United Nations Educational, Scientific, and Cultural Organization. On the left is the Ecole Militaire.

UNIVERSITE PIERRE ET MARIE CURIE

Seen from above the Seine is the Université Pierre et Marie
Curie. Its tower partly obscures the Place Jussieu. Beyond and
to the right is the Arènes de Lutèce.

SAINT-GERMAIN-DES-PRES

(Opposite) The Boulevard Saint-Germain runs through the historic left bank of the Seine, district of Saint-Germain-des-Prés, once a farming area outside Paris. Saint-Germain-des-Prés became the site of aristocratic mansions of pre-revolutionary times. Before and after World War II, it was the favorite hangout of the Parisian and foreign intelligentsia.

Now a popular place for students and tourists, it is dotted with small cafés and bistros. The area is also filled with beautiful churches, one of which is the basilica of Sainte-Clotilde, (top right) built in 1857, in the neo-gothic style.

THE VAL-DE-GRACE

The Val-de-Grâce, the Abbey and Church of which were built in the seventeenth century, is now a medical center and a site for higher education. The Val-de-Grâce includes a museum devoted to military medicine.

PALAIS-ROYAL

Little remains today of the original Palais-Royal, the work of Cardinal de Richelieu in the seventeenth century. From him, it passed into the hands of royalty. In 1661, Moliere and his troupe played in a theater in the Palais-Royal. Just before the Revolution, Philippe d'Orleans built 60 pavilions around three sides of the Palais, which later became boutiques. After the Revolution, the Palais was turned into a gambling and dancing hall. In 1836, it was closed. Today, it houses only the Conseil d'Etat (the Council of State) and the Ministry of Culture. The gardens of the Palais were designed in the eighteenth century.

THE LOUVRE

(Opposite) The Louvre is the largest and one of the most extraordinary palaces in the world. It started as a fortress around the year 1200. The buildings of today's actual Louvre were started in 1546 under Francois I. Construction proceeded during the following years under a succession of monarchs. The final work was done by Napoléon III. After the French Revolution, the Convention decided to turn the Louvre into a museum. At that time, it contained 650 art objects; today, the number is 400,000. It has one of the most valuable art collections in the world.

In 1564, Catherine di Medici started to build a castle opposite the Louvre and between it and the Place de la Concorde of today. But her Tuileries Palace was destroyed during the uprising of the Paris Commune in 1871. As a result, there is now an exceptionally straight line which exists between the Louvre and the Arc de Triomphe and which passes through the garden of the Tuileries, the Place de la Concorde, and the Champs-Elysées.

THE SORBONNE

The Sorbonne, the most prestigious institution of higher education in France, is situated on the left bank of the Seine. It was originally founded in the mid-thirteenth century as a school for poor students. The construction of the present complex was directed by Cardinal de Richelieu in the seventeenth century. Suppressed by the Revolution, the Sorbonne and the University of Paris were reopened by Napoléon. Extensive rebuilding and additions to the complex took place at the end of the nineteenth century and at the beginning of the twentieth century.

The Sorbonne was the center of the student riots in May, 1968. These riots, which paralyzed France, became known as the "Events of May" and led to an extensive reform of the French system of higher education. The Sorbonne Church, in the center, was erected between 1635 and 1642. The tomb of Cardinal de Richelieu is in the church.

SAINT-SULPICE

(Opposite) Saint-Sulpice was once a parish church for the peasants living outside Paris in Saint-Germain-des-Prés. It was constructed in the sixteenth, seventeenth and eighteenth centuries. On the far right, you can see the Palais du Luxembourg, the seat of the French Senate.

65

THE PALAIS DU LUXEMBOURG

The Palais du Luxembourg was built in the early seventeenth century for Marie di Medici, the widow of Henri IV, and was decorated with large paintings by Rubens. These works are now in the Louvre. The palace remained with the royal family until the Revolution when it was converted to a prison. Since 1800, it has been the site of the upper house of the French Legislature, named the Senate in 1852 by Napoléon III. On the left is the Petit Luxembourg, the home of the President of the Senate. The expansive gardens at the rear of the palace were also designed during the time of Marie di Medici.

THE ARCHIVES

(Opposite) Soon after the French Revolution, the historic Archives of France were placed in the Hôtel Soubise (in the foreground). Built in 1705, the hotel also contains the Historical Museum of France. The Hôtel de Rohan (behind the Hôtel Soubise) became an annex for the Archives in 1927.

GARE MONTPARNASSE—TOUR MONTPARNASSE

Rising 688 feet from behind one of Paris' most important railroad stations is the Tour Montparnasse. Completed in 1973, it is the tallest building in Paris. From the restaurant and bar on the 56th floor, there is a spectacular view of Paris. On the left, in the rear, one can see the Invalides.

THE OBSERVATORY

The four walls of the Observatory, constructed in 1667, are oriented to the points of the compass. Within the Observatory are the International Time Bureau, which sets Coordinated Universal Time, and a speaking clock, which can be reached by telephone. This clock is accurate to one-fiftieth of a second. In the background is the Palais du Luxembourg, the seat of the French Senate.

ECOLE MILITAIRE

The Ecole Militaire (military school), completed in 1772, now houses a number of the higher schools of French National Defense and schools of Advanced War Studies attended by French and allied officers. On the right is another view of the Ecole Militaire with the Invalides in the background.

BOULEVARD SAINT-GERMAIN

In the seventh arrondissement at lower right, we get a glimpse of the National Assembly and above it is Sainte-Clotilde. At center, the modern building is the Ministry of Defense in the Boulevard Saint-Germain.

SAINT-SÉVERIN AND SAINT-JULIEN-LE-PAUVRE

(Opposite) The church of Saint-Séverin was begun in the sixth century. It became a parish church for the left bank of the Seine in the eleventh century, when the area was mostly farmland. The present Gothic church, on this same site, was begun in the middle of the thirteenth century.

On the bottom, at the right, is the church of Saint-Julien-le-Pauvre, which has been located here since the third century. The present building, which replaced the old church, was constructed between the twelfth and thirteenth centuries.

NATIONAL ASSEMBLY

The National Assembly, the lower house of the French Legislature, is installed in an historic building called the Palais Bourbon. The original building on the property was built in the early eighteenth century by the Duchess of Bourbon, a daughter of Louis XIV. It was enlarged and embellished during the reigns of Louis XV and Louis XVI. The Palace was confiscated during the Revolution and used as a meeting place for the Council of 500.

In 1827, the palace was converted to its present function, as the home of the National Assembly. Made up of 491 members, the National Assembly has virtually all of the legislative power in France. Very little power is in the hands of the Senate, as it cannot stop laws from being adopted; it can only delay them. The present façade of the National Assembly was commissioned by Napoléon in 1807 to match the Greek style of the Madeleine across the Seine. Behind the National Assembly is the Place du Palais Bourbon. In the foreground is the Seine River.

BOTANICAL GARDENS

(Opposite) Depicted here are the Paris Botanical Gardens (Jardin des Plantes) on the banks of the Seine. Behind them are the modern buildings of the Pierre and Marie Curie University. On the right is a more complete view of the university.

THE PALAIS DE JUSTICE

This complex on the Ile de la Cité includes the Palais de Justice (the Hall of Justice), the Sainte-Chapelle and the Conciergerie. The Palais de Justice is on the site of an earlier Palace, once inhabited by Charlemagne. It was as early as the fifteenth century that justice began to be administered there, but the building did not become the Palais de Justice until the Revolution. The Conciergerie in the foreground, used to house the Concierge or administrator of the Royal Palace. It was during the Revolution that the Conciergerie played its most historic role, as a prison for some 2,600 aristocrats and others, who were later guillotined.

Queen Marie-Antoinette spent the last thirty-five days of her life there before being beheaded on October 16, 1793. The Sainte-Chapelle in the courtyard of what is now the Palais de Justice is a thirteenth century jewel of stained-glass windows. At the right are views of the Palais de Justice, of the Conciergerie, and of all that is left of the Tour Saint-Jacques. Built in the sixteenth century, the Tour Saint-Jacques was one of the starting points for pilgrims on their trip to Santiago de Compostela. Today, it houses a meteorologic station.

CANAL ST-MARTIN

The Canal St-Martin runs for about three miles from the Ourcq Canal to the Seine River. It is heavily travelled by some 4000 barges a year. On the far right is the St-Louis Hospital, built in the seventeenth century when Paris was hit by the plague.

THE ARENES DE LUTECE

(Opposite) The arena in the center of the picture is one of the few remaining signs of the Gallo-Roman occupation of Paris. There were several arenas on this site; thus, it is called the Arènes de Lutece. The arenas were destroyed in the third century B.C. and remained buried until 1869, when they were discovered during the building of a road. The arena above has been restored along with its ancient stone tiers which have been preserved.

THE PARC MONCEAU

Originally conceived of by the Duke of Chartres in 1778, the Parc Monceau is one of the more beautiful green areas of Paris. In the foreground is a rotunda, called the Pavillon de Chartres. Designed in the neoclassical style by the eighteenth century architect, Nicholas Ledoux, it is a rare survivor of the customs houses which surrounded Paris before the Revolution.

ROTONDE DE LA VILLETTE

(Opposite) The Rotonde de la Villette is one of fifty-seven customs houses which composed part of a wall built around Paris between 1784 and 1791. The waterway in the foreground is the Bassin de la Villette. In the background is the Canal St-Martin.

BUTTES-CHAUMONT

It was once a garbage dump and a gathering place for tramps. Now the Buttes-Chaumont has been transformed into a beautiful 166-acre park, with a 5-acre lake which gets its water supply from the Canal Saint-Martin. The inauguration of the Buttes-Chaumont took place in 1867.

THE PERE LACHAISE

(Opposite) The Père Lachaise was purchased in 1626 by the Jesuits. It was Father de la Chaise, the personal confessor of Louis XIV, who erected the first buildings there. In 1763, the Jesuits were expelled. In 1803, the property was transformed into Paris' largest cemetery. During the revolt of the Paris Commune in 1871, the cemetery was the site of the bloodiest fighting. Among those buried there are the singer, Edith Piaf; the writers, Colette and Oscar Wilde; the composer, Georges Bizet; and the painters, Modigliani and Cobot.

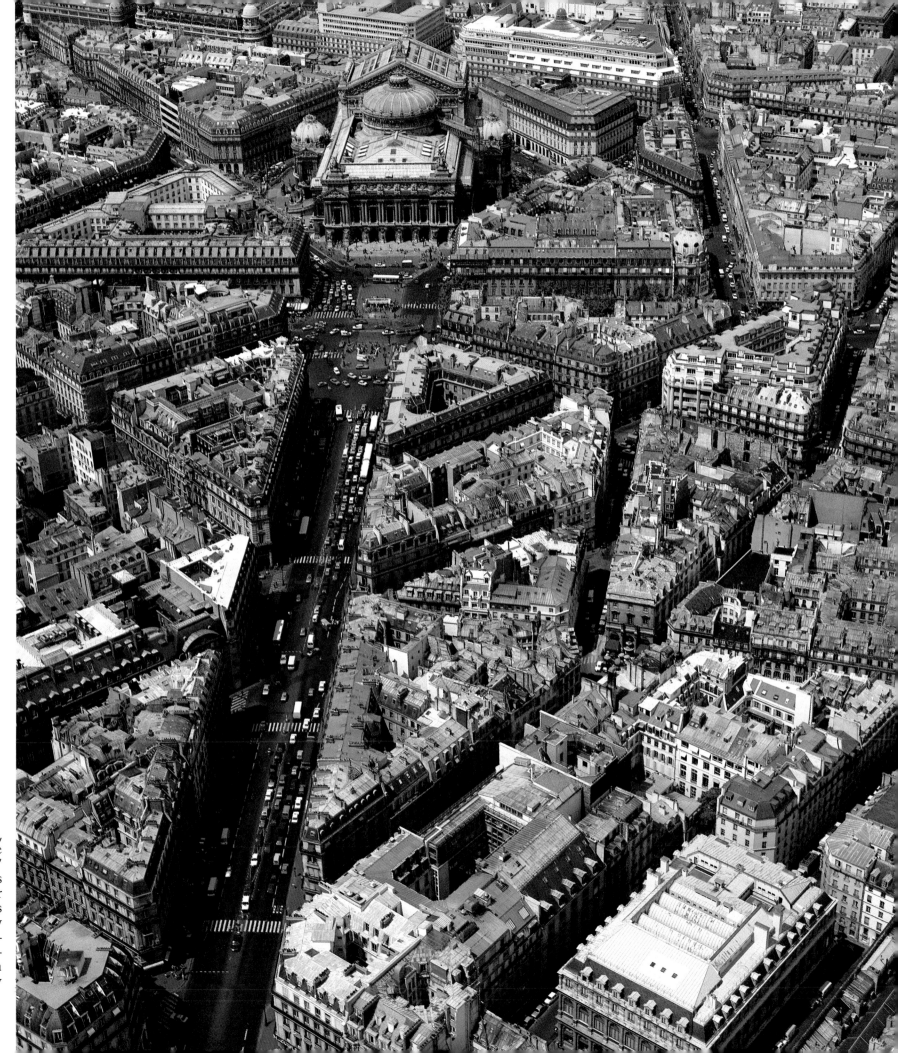

AVENUE DE L'OPERA—OPERA

In the foreground is the Avenue de l'Opéra, carved into the city in the middle of the nineteenth century. It is now one of Paris' streets of distinction. In the background is the Paris Opera—named the Palais Garnier after its thirty-five year old architect, Charles Garnier. Started in 1862, the Opera finally opened in 1875. The Paris Opera has the largest stage in the world which can accommodate 450 artists. The inside is dominated by a six-ton chandelier and a 1964 painting by Chagall which is on the ceiling.

ARC DE TRIOMPHE

The Arc de Triomphe has always been an important point in Paris from which avenues branched off in many directions. It was not until 1758, that someone suggested building a monument there. An engineer, named Ribart, proposed building a giant elephant topped by a statue of Louis XV, with water gushing from the trunk of the elephant. It never happened. In 1806, just after the victory of the Battle of Austerlitz, Napoléon proposed building an arc of triumph to honor France's victorious armies. When Napoléon fell in 1814, the Arc de Triomphe was only partly built. The Arc was finally completed between 1832 and 1836. It was covered with

sculptures to illustrate the great moments of the French Empire and of the French Revolution.

These exceptional aerial photographs clearly show the avenues branching out of the Place Charles De Gaulle (previously named, l'Etoile—the Star) on which the Arc de Triomphe stands. Other than the Champs-Elysées, some of the more famous avenues emanating from the Arc are the Avenue Foch, the Avenue de la Grande Armée, and the Avenue Marceau, where one can see the Saint-Pierre-de-Chaillot Church.

AVENUE FOCH

(Opposite) The Avenue Foch is one of the most beautiful avenues in Paris. It was created in 1854 and origi-·nally named the Avenue de l'Impératrice. Its purpose was to provide a particularly stately passage from the Étoile to the Bois de Boulogne. It is the broadest avenue in Paris. In 1929, it received its present name to honor the Maréchal Foch, a French hero of World War I. The apartments which line the Avenue Foch house the most wealthy of the Parisian population.

AVENUE MARCEAU

Avenue Marceau bends its elegant way from lower right to the Etoile where
a frieze on the Arc de Triomphe depicts General Marceau's funeral.

MADELEINE

This view shows the Church of the Madeleine in the foreground. To the rear, on the left, is the Gare St. Lazare, the railroad station which links Paris to the suburbs and to Normandy. In the middle, on the right, is the roof of the Paris Opera.

BOULEVARD DE LA MADELEINE

The Boulevard de la Madeleine is one of a number of "Grands Boulevards" or great boulevards in Paris. Originally traced in 1680, it derives its present name from the fact that it runs to the Madeleine Church, which is in the background. On the left is the Place de la Concorde.

THE PLACE DU TROCADERO

(Opposite) The Place du Trocadéro, completed in 1858, is dominated by a statue of Maréchal Foch, the French hero of World War I. In the foreground are the Palais de Chaillot, built in 1937, which contains the Museum of Man, the Maritime Museum, the Henri Langlois Cinema Museum, the French Cinémathèque, one of the most complete and presti-gious film archives in the world and the People's National Theater, which seats 1,800 persons. Out of the Trocadéro flow arteries leading to the Iéna bridge, the Arc de Triomphe, the Bois de Boulogne, and Porte Maillot, with its convention center, the Palais des Congrès.

THE MOULIN DE LA GALETTE

(Opposite) The Moulin (Windmill) de la Galette, which dates back to the fifteenth century, stands in the middle of the Montmartre section of Paris. It served as an inspiration for many painters including Renoir and Van Gogh.

PORTE MAILLOT

The Porte Maillot, on the west end of Paris, with the giant Palais des Congrès, is used as a convention center and also as a large hall for ballets, operas, and concerts.

SACRE-COEUR

On a clear day, you can see the Sacré-Coeur (the Sacred Heart) from 40 miles away. It stands at the top of the Montmartre district as a monument which dominates Paris.

After France's crushing defeat by the Germans in the War of 1870, the National Assembly, pushed by the important Roman Catholic lobby in France, decided, as a sign of hope, to build the Basilica of the Sacré-Coeur. The design chosen produced a white church which looked like a huge wedding cake. Much of it was paid for by the public, that is, those of whom could contribute enough money to buy a stone, a pillar, or a column. Construction of the Sacré-Coeur began in 1875. Although it was officially dedicated in 1891, it was not actually completed until 1919. In 1895, a giant chariot pulled by more than 20 teams of oxen delivered the 19-ton bell, called the Savoyarde, to the church, where it was installed under the campanile.

The Sacré-Coeur has become a tremendous tourist attraction. It can be reached by walking up the long set of stairs to the church, or by taking the funicular which is to the left of the stairs. From the Sacré-Coeur, one gets an extraordinary view of Paris and of the Montmartre district, famous for its artists and outdoor cafés. Next to the Sacré-Coeur, one can see the smaller, beautiful church of Saint-Pierre-de-Montmartre, one of the oldest in Paris, as it was started in 1134.

MONTMARTRE

In the foreground of the Montmartre section of Paris can be seen the church of Saint-Jean-l'Evangéliste built between 1894 and 1904.

SACRE-COEUR

(Opposite) This evening photo exemplifies the characterization of Paris as the "City of Light." In the foreground are lighted Bateaux-Mouches, preparing for a trip down the river. In the background, bathed by the rays of the falling sun, is the Sacré-Coeur. To the right is the same scene in daylight.

SIXTEENTH ARRONDISSEMENT

(Opposite) This view of the wealthy sixteenth arrondissement of Paris is seen with the Porte de St-Cloud in the foreground. On the left is the modern church of Sainte-Jeanne-de-Chantal. In the background, at the left, is the Longchamp race track.

BIBLIOTHEQUE NATIONALE

The national library (Bibliothèque Nationale) was moved seven times before it was finally installed in the Maison Tubeuf in 1720. It includes, today, nearly 9,000,000 volumes, among which are two Bibles printed by Gutenberg. It has collections of coins and stamps and the most important collections of prints and photographs in the world. Among the volumes included are books and manuscripts seized during the Revolution from abbeys, convents, and other ecclesiastical institutions. In the background are the gardens of the Palais-Royal.

LA VILLETTE

La Villette was once the site of Paris' slaughterhouses. Under construction in this location is a museum of Science and Technology and what is to become the French capital's most important music hall.

GARE DE LYON

(Opposite) If you are going south to the Cote d'Azur, you can catch your train at the Gare de Lyon, which has one of Paris' best restaurants, "Le Train Bleu." In the foreground is the Paris-Bercy Omnisports Palace, opened in 1983 by the municipality of Paris as a giant sports center. It has been the basis of one of Paris' strong arguments to be the host of the 1992 Olympic Games.

RITZ HOTEL

Here is a unique view of the esteemed Ritz Hotel in the Place Vendôme. Founded by Cesar Ritz in 1898, it is, today, the symbol of the elegance and of the style of the French luxury hotels. It has been lavishly restored by its new owner, Mohammed Al Fayed. Legend has it that the Ritz was "liberated" from the Germans by the American writer, Ernest Hemingway, at the end of World War II.

BOURSE

(Opposite) The Paris stock exchange, or Bourse, was built on the former site of the convent of the Filles St-Thomas. The original building, designed by the architect Brongniart, was constructed between 1808 and 1827; it was enlarged in 1907 and now has the shape of a latin cross. Its four corners display statuary evoking Commerce, Agriculture, Industry and Commercial Law. Across the street on rue Quatre-Septembre are the offices of the news organization Agence France-Presse.

BELLEVILLE
Depicted is the modern Belleville section in
the east of Paris near the Buttes-Chaumont.

QUARTIER D'ITALIE
(Opposite) Depicted here is the modern complex
which has grown up near the Porte d'Italie in the
southern sector of Paris. In the background, the Tour
Montparnasse, the highest building in Paris, towers
over the other structures.

THE ENVIRONS

VINCENNES

The Bois de Vincennes, the former Bondy Forest, at the left, was renovated under Napoléon III. It now contains a zoo, a race track, an amusement park, and a number of artificial lakes.

On the following pages, stand the Royal Castle of Vincennes, the first part of which was completed in 1370. The Cardinal Mazarin, who became governor of Vincennes, added to the castle in the seventeenth century. During the Revolution, the mobs attempted to destroy the castle, but it was saved by the Marquis de La Fayette, a hero of the American Revolution. Napoléon converted the castle to an arsenal in the early nineteenth century and had the towers in the corners destroyed. On August 24, 1944, the day before the liberation of Paris, the Germans, who were occupying the castle, shot 25 resistance fighters and set off three mines which damaged the King's Pavilion and set fire to the Queen's Pavilion.

MEUDON

Near Meudon is France's most important astronomical observatory, created in 1876. The mushroom-like top was added in 1965. In the seventeenth century, Monseigneur, the son of Louis XIV, who owned a château nearby, hunted wolves on this property. The château, neglected after the French Revolution, was razed in 1804.

LA DEFENSE

The decision in 1958 to transform a 2000 acre site, just west of Paris, into a new urban office and living area produced the largest construction job in the history of the Paris region. The results were: 30 skyscrapers, underground shopping centers, accesses to mass transit, and a number of colorful high-rise apartments (see photograph above). Some 50,000 persons work and live in La Défense. Their link to Paris is clear, as one can see the Arc de Triomphe in the background. Between the office building and the apartments is a park dedicated to the memory of the French writer, André Malraux. Among the buildings, stand statues produced by modern artists, such as Calder and Miro.

LONGCHAMP

The Longchamp race track was inaugurated by Napoléon III in 1857. There was an abbey on the left side of the course, but, it was destroyed by the Revolution. All that remains is the rebuilt windmill. Longchamp is the site of Europe's most prestigious race, the *Arc de Triomphe*, held each year on the first Sunday in October.

AUTEUIL

(Opposite) The Auteuil race track, on the edge of the Bois de Boulogne, is the site of France's best steeplechasing.

BAGATELLE

(Opposite) Once the property of the French royalty, Bagatelle is now a beautiful garden inside the Bois de Boulogne.

THE RACING CLUB DE FRANCE

The most eminent sporting organization in France, the Racing Club de France, was founded in 1882. Its main facilities are in the Bois de Boulogne.

CERCLE DU BOIS DE BOULOGNE

The Cercle du Bois de Boulogne is a private
club in the forest which specializes in tennis
and skeet shooting.

NEUILLY

(Opposite) Neuilly-sur-Seine, to the west of
Paris, is the richest of the city's suburbs.

LA BOULIE AND SAINT-CLOUD

France has beautiful golf courses and has produced some international champions. On the left is La Boulie, the golf courses of the Racing Club of France. On the right is Saint-Cloud, the site of the annual French Open Golf Tournament which was being played when this photograph was made.

RENAULT

Founded in 1898, the Renault auto company has developed into one of the largest in Europe. Its principal plant in Billancourt, on the western rim of Paris, occupies both sides of the Seine and the Seguin island in the middle of the river. Thirty thousand people work there.

PARC DES PRINCES AND ROLAND GARROS

(Opposite) In the background is the Parc des Princes, Paris' largest sports stadium. It is the site of French and European soccer and rugby matches. In the foreground is the Roland Garros tennis stadium which is the site of the annual French Open, one of the four most important tennis tournaments in the world.

ECOLE POLYTECHNIQUE

(Opposite) The new and modern Ecole Polytechnique in Palaiseau is one of the two or three most highly respected schools in France. Polytechnique was founded in 1794 as a training ground for engineers destined to direct public works after the French Revolution. In 1804, Napoléon gave the school a military statute, and the training was expanded to include military engineering. Today's modern site is a far cry from the historic buildings which the school previously occupied in the center of Paris.

T.G.V.

One of France's most remarkable technological advances, the T.G.V. (Train à Grande Vitesse), whips through the French countryside at more than 200 miles per hour.

ORLY-CHARLES DE GAULLE

On the left is Orly West Airport to the south of Paris. It is used almost exclusively for internal French flights. It was opened in 1971. On the right is Charles de Gaulle No. 1, a more recent airport north of Paris. This airport is reserved for international flights by foreign airlines. In the background, one can see Paris' latest airport, Charles de Gaulle No. 2, reserved exclusively for Air France national and international flights. It is from there that the Concorde leaves for its daily flight to New York.

ILE DE FRANCE

CHAMPS

(Opposite) The eighteenth century Château de Champs, built by a French financier, is most noted for its gardens, considered to be among the most beautiful in France. Once the residence of the charismatic Madame de Pompadour, it now houses the workshops where the treasures of French museums are restored.

ILE DE FRANCE

The region around Paris is called the Ile de France. Its classic beauty has been enjoyed since the time of the Celts.

Despite the ravages of the French Revolution, hundreds of castles, built from the twelfth to the nineteenth century, remain standing. Many of them, for example, Versailles and Fontainebleau, have become exquisite museums.

To visit the Ile de France is to experience some of the glories and grandeur of earlier times.

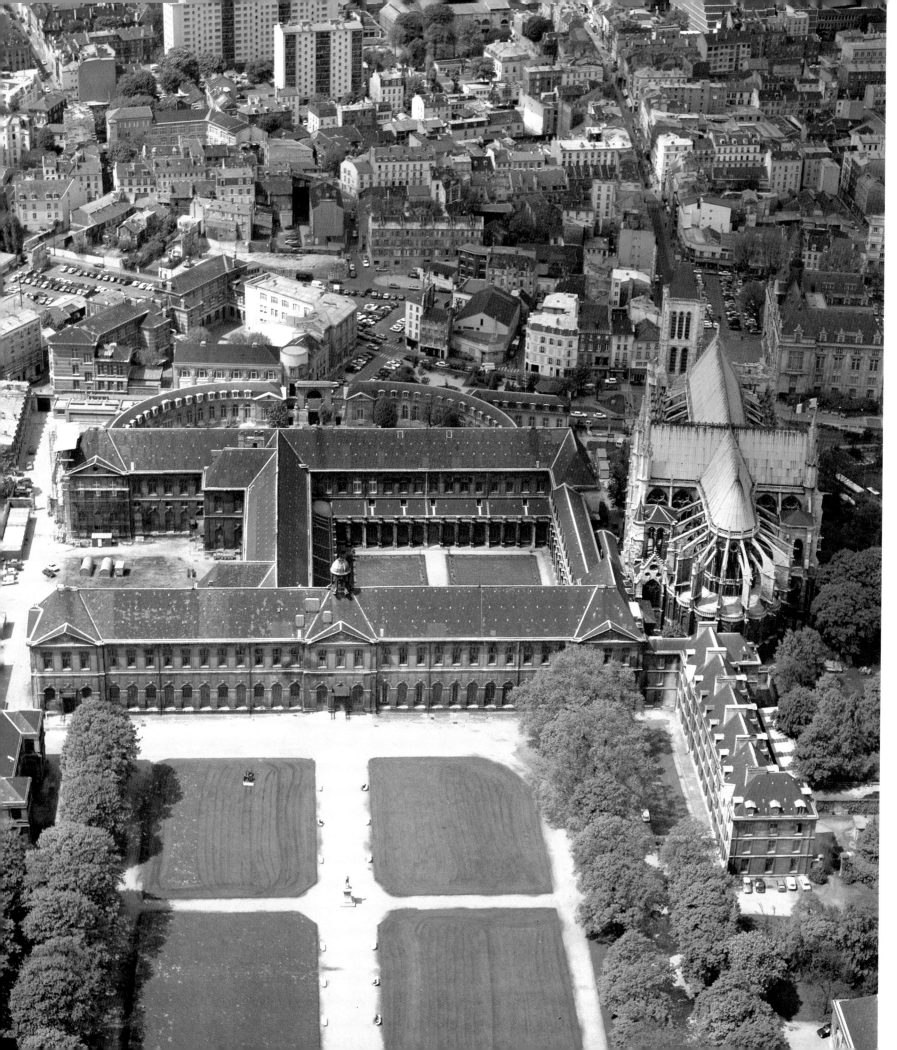

SAINT-DENIS

The Basilica of Saint-Denis, which is located in a working class district in the north of Paris, was constructed in the twelfth century by the Abbot Suger. The Basilica was restored in the nineteenth century. At one time, it was the burial ground of kings, queens, and other royalty of France. But the tombs were desecrated during the French Revolution. Connected to the church is an ancient abbey, built in the eighteenth century and converted by Napoléon to a school for young daughters of members of the Legion of Honor.

SAINT-GERMAIN-EN-LAYE

(Opposite) The Château Vieux de Saint-Germain-en-Laye was built by François I to control the roads to Normandy. Because Henri III was displeased with the Château Vieux, he built the Château Neuf only to have it destroyed later by Charles X. Today, the Château Vieux houses the National Museum of Antiquities.

CHATEAU DE FONTAINEBLEAU

(Opposite) The Château de Fontainebleau, one of the largest royal residences in France, is deeply rooted in the history of the country. François I started building the castle in the sixteenth century. Subsequently, many other monarchs left their marks on Fontainebleau. Much of the original construction was completed by famous Italian artisans. It was here, at Fontainebleau, that Napoléon made his farewell speech to his troops in the Cour des Adieux, before being exiled on the island of Elba. And, it was here, in 1984, that the heads of state and the governments of the European Community met and finally resolved the European Economic Community's (E.E.C.) nagging budget dispute.

MAISONS-LAFFITTE

The Château de Maisons-Laffitte was built between 1642 and 1651 near the Seine River. The opulent party, which heralded the opening of the castle, was attended by Louis XIV, when he was just thirteen years old. The Count d'Artois, the brother of Louis XVI, bought the Château in 1777 and built the famous Maisons-Laffitte racetrack nearby. In the early nineteenth century, the Château became the gathering place for leading French political figures including the Marquis de La Fayette, a hero of the American Revolution.

FERRIERES

The Château de Ferrières was built in the mid-nineteenth century by James de Rothschild, who was then the head of the French contingent of the famed European Rothschild banking family. Napoléon III attended the opening party there in 1862. Bismark lived at Ferrières while his German troops engaged in the siege of Paris during the War of 1870.

In this century, it has been the site of lavish costume balls given by the Baron Guy de Rothschild and his wife Marie-Hélène. In 1777, the Rothschilds donated Ferrières to the Chancellery of the University of Paris.

LES VAUX DE CERNAY

(Opposite) Les Vaux de Cernay, a twelfth century Cistercian Abbey, was partially destroyed during the French Revolution. In 1873, the property was purchased by the Baronne Nathaniel de Rothschild, who restored it to its present state.

PORT ROYAL

What is left of the Abbey of Port Royal des Champs, near Versailles, is more a memorial to new ideas than to old buildings. It was once a complex made up of an abbey and a school, which attracted the free spirits of the time. The most well-known of the students was the French writer, Jean Racine. Also attracted there was Blaise Pascal, a scientific genius of his era. The school and the abbey of Port Royal produced a theological, as well as moralistic, tempest in France which Louis XIV saw as a challenge to his influence. In 1709, the complex was closed. But, it still remains as a hallowed site for those who believe in the freedom of thought and of speech.

BRETEUIL

The Château de Breteuil was built over a period of three centuries and was finally finished in the nineteenth century. It has been in the hands of the Breteuil family since 1712 and can be rented for parties or picnics.

135

DAMPIERRE

The Château de Dampierre, built in 1680 on the site of a Renaissance palace, sits in a symmetrical garden designed by the famous Le Nôtre. The interior of the Château is considered one of the most beautiful in France, and it contains a royal apartment that was inhabited successively by Louis XIV, XV, and XVI.

GALLARDON

(Opposite) People have been waiting for more than 500 years for this tower, partly damaged in 1443, to collapse. But, what is left still stands and is called "L'épaule de Gallardon." The guide book suggests that you see it from as far away as possible. This aerial photograph is probably the best way to see this ancient oddity. Behind it is a church which was first built in the twelfth century, with further additions later.

MORTEFONTAINE

(Opposite) Once the home of Joseph Bonaparte and Caroline Murat, the Château of Mortefontaine and its beautiful surroundings also served as an inspiration to the great French painter, Corot, and to the celebrated French poet, Gérard de Nerval.

RAMBOUILLET

It was in the Château de Rambouillet, built in 1375, that François I died in 1547. Down through the centuries, many French monarchs came to this magnificent castle to hunt or to live. The English gardens of the castle were designed in the eighteenth century. It is from the Château de Rambouillet that General de Gaulle, who was living there from August 23 to 25, 1944, gave the orders for the final assault to liberate Paris. It was here that the first summit of the seven industrialized nations of the world took place in 1974 under the presidency of Valéry Giscard d'Estaing.

ROYAUMONT

Founded in 1235 by St. Louis, the Abbaye de Royaumont, minus its church which was destroyed during the French Revolution, is one of the many religious structures constructed by the Cistercians. It now belongs to the Royaumont Foundation and is used for seminars, study groups, and concerts. It has a superb garden, surrounded by the cloisters.

ECOUEN

(Opposite) Built between 1538 and 1555, the Château d'Ecouen now belongs to the French Ministry of Culture and houses the National Museum of the Renaissance. At one time, it was a school for the daughters of members of the Legion of Honor. The Château is an example of the architecture of the Second Renaissance.

VOISINS

This magnificent Château de Voisins, with its expansive, manicured gardens, its lake, and its river must have been a joy to the royalty who built it in the eighteenth century outside of Paris. It is so private, as it is surrounded by the trees of the thick forest. The architectural style of this massive structure is Neo-Grecian.

ESCLIMONT

(Opposite) The Château d'Esclimont was built in 1543 for the Archbishop of Tours. The Renaissance facade was added in the nineteenth century. It is now a château-hotel.

ANET

What we see today is only a part of the spectacular Château of Anet built in the sixteenth century. Large portions of the Château were destroyed in the eighteenth century. It was built for Diane de Poitiers, a longtime mistress of Henri II.

COURANCES

(Opposite) The surrounding forests, gardens, and ponds make the Château de Courances particularly attractive. It was built in 1550. In the nineteenth century, an imitation of the horseshoe stairway of the Château de Fontainebleau was added to the front.

145

SENLIS

This city is one of the oldest in France and survived the days of the Romans and of the Barbarians. Senlis has the look of a fortress town, because the 350-yard Gallo-Roman fortification, which once surrounded it, has been replaced by houses.

The photograph above is a closer view of the Notre-Dame

Cathedral of Senlis. Construction of this Cathedral started in 1153, just ten years before work began on the Notre-Dame in Paris. After being partially destroyed by lightning in 1504, the Notre-Dame Cathedral of Senlis was rebuilt in its present form.

CHANTILLY

Chantilly is more than several castles and a beautiful race track; it is one of the most beautiful monuments to France's historic past. It is intriguing that the first castle was built there 2,000 years ago. The large Chantilly Château is a nineteenth century imitation of the Renaissance style. The smaller château is an authentic structure of the French Renaissance. Horse racing started there in 1834. The stables were built to house 240 horses.

Formerly well-known for its lace and porcelain manufacture and as the residence of the Condés, Chantilly is even more celebrated now for its château and the annual race of the Jockey Club. The park and the castle (now comprising an important museum) were bequeathed to the Institut de France by the duc d'Aumale in 1886 along with his library and art collection.

VÉTHEUIL

The French painter, Monet, was so captivated by the beauty of Vétheuil, that he lived there for three years. Situated on the Seine, its centerpiece is a church, started in the twelfth century, which took four centuries to finish. In older times, Vétheuil was a village populated by wine growers.

ERMENONVILLE

(Opposite) Ermenonville, with its château, lovely lakes, and forests, is dedicated to the memory of Jean-Jacques Rousseau, France's celebrated philosopher. His tomb can be seen in the foreground of the picture. In 1794, his remains, like those of many other famous Frenchmen, were transferred to the Panthéon in Paris.

CHAALIS

Chaâlis is located near the Ermenonville forest. It was originally constructed as an Abbey in 1136. In succeeding years, it was virtually abandoned. Finally, in 1850, a woman bought it and transformed it into a castle, surrounded by superb gardens. Today, Chaâlis is the property of the French Institute.

VERSAILLES

The Château de Versailles is the most striking reminder of the power and wealth of the French royalty in the seventeenth and eighteenth centuries. It is the place from which France was ruled for a little more than a century (1682 to 1789), by the Bourbon Dynasty. It was the fulfillment of a dream for Louis XIV. The building of Versailles took 22,000 workers and some of the best artists of the time. The construction lasted almost 50 years.

The complex is made up of the Château, its orangerie (orange grove), the Grand Trianon, the Petit Trianon, and more than 250 acres of lavish gardens. All of this has been mostly restored due to the work of its former curator, Gerald Van Der Kemp (now the curator of Giverny) and his American-born wife, and through contributions, for the most part, by Americans.

On the following page is a view of the Grand Trianon (part of Versailles), the favorite "country house" of Louis XIV, who liked to go there, sometimes by boat, with the women of his life.

On the left is an unusual view of the Versailles complex, behind the city of Versailles.

GROS BOIS

The Château de Gros Bois, built under Henri IV and Louis XIII, became the home of the Maréchal Berthier during the Empire of Napoléon. Berthier decorated it with paintings depicting the glory of Napoléon's victories. The Château is a marvelous example of the mixture of stone and brick.

GRIGNON

The Château de Grignon was built during the reign of Louis XIII and restored under Napoléon. It is now the National Agronomic Center. It was formerly called either the Royal School of Agriculture or the Imperial School of Agriculture depending upon the preference of the person in power at the time.

LA ROCHE-GUYON

The Château de La Roche-Guyon was started in the thirteenth century. Building and rebuilding continued until its completion in the eighteenth century. The Château sits on the rise that comes up from the Seine River. Perhaps more interesting is the fortress behind it which was built in the eleventh century.

MER DE SABLE

You are only 30 miles from Paris, in the forest of Ermenonville, but, looking at it from the air, you would think you were over the Sahara Desert. Yet, this oddity, called Mer de Sable, is one of the favorite spots in France for young children who love riding on a small train which crosses the some 70-acres of sand. And, across the road, to add to the outing's entertainment, is a small zoo.

158

GIVERNY

(Opposite) The French Impressionist painter, Claude Monet, bought Giverny in 1890 after having lived there for some time. In 1914, he had a new studio built there. Many of Monet's paintings, including the *Water Lilies,* were inspired by these beautiful gardens. Giverny was recently restored and converted to a public museum with the help of a generous gift from Lila Acheson Wallace.

CREDITS

Bibliothèque Historique de la Ville de Paris
    Melle Hélène Verlet
    Mme. Marie de Thézy
    M. Jean-Marc Leri

and for the great cooperation of:
    M. Jean Derens

Musée Carnavalet
    Melle Françoise Reynaud

Caisse Nationale des Monuments Historiques
    M. Jean-Jacques Poulet-Allamagny

Musée Marmottan
    Mme. Marianne Delafond

Archives Nationales
    Mme. Nicole Felkay

Etablissement Public pour l'Amenagement de la Défense
    Mme. Catherine Le Morellec

l'Illustration

And for very special assistance from the
    Mme. Roxane Debuisson Collection.

BIBLIOGRAPHY

Dictionnaire des Rues de Paris—Jacques Hillairet
Dictionnaire de Paris—Larousse Publishers
Paris et les Parisiens—Robert Laffont Publishers
Histoire de Paris—René Héron de Villefosse
Construction de Paris—René Héron de Villefosse
Paris Histoire Illustrée—Gabrielle Wittkop,
                  Justus Franz Wittkop
Paris: a Century of Change (1878-1978) Norma Evenson
Paris—Henri Bidou
Paris Monumental—Flammarion Publishers
Michelin Green Guide on Paris
Paris aux Cent Villages—(monthly magazine)
Michelin Green Guide on Ile de France
Les Environs de Paris aujourd'hui—Paulette Crottès
Guide de l'Ile de France Mystérieuse—Tchou Publishers
Jardins de France—Ernest de Ganay
Hommage à Claude Monet—Catalogue of the Exhibition
                  at the Grand Palais, 1980

MAINTENON (*Photograph on page 4*)

The Château de Maintenon, located thirty-four miles southwest of Versailles, was built in the fifteenth century on the foundation of a medieval fortress. It was given by Louis XIV to his second wife. The water in front of the castle flows in from the Eure River, and, in the foreground is located one of the most colossal projects of the period; that is, an aqueduct which was to be 5,000 yards long and 75 yards high.

VAUX-LE-VICOMTE (*Photograph on page 5*)

It took 18,000 of the period's best artisans five years to build, what many consider to be, the most beautiful of the seventeenth century castles: namely, Vaux-le-Vicomte.

Fouquet, who had been prosecutor General of Paris, and later, the top assistant of Mazarin at the Ministry of Finance, built Vaux-le-Vicomte. Fouquet made the mistake of inviting King Louis XIV to a lavish party at his castle. The King became envious because his castle was less grand. He proceeded to arrest Fouquet and to take possession of Vaux-le-Vicomte. Not yet satisfied, he took the 18,000 artisans and had them build a sumptuous palace at Versailles to surpass the other castles. Fouquet's wife later succeeded in having Vaux-le-Vicomte returned to her. It survived the French Revolution with little damage and remains today, one of the privately-owned wonders of France.